A **TRUMP** DIARY

HOW I SUFFERED THROUGH THE BULL$%#&,
TALKED MYSELF DOWN, AND SURVIVED
THE FIRST YEAR OF THE APOCALYPSE.

S. TIMOTHY **GLASSCOCK**

authorHOUSE®

AuthorHouse™
1663 Liberty Drive
Bloomington, IN 47403
www.authorhouse.com
Phone: 1 (800) 839-8640

Published by AuthorHouse 03/08/2019

ISBN: 978-1-7283-0227-0 (sc)
ISBN: 978-1-7283-0226-3 (e)

Print information available on the last page.

This book is printed on acid-free paper.

Scripture taken from The Holy Bible, King James Version. Public Domain

FOREWORD

On November 8, 2016, Donald J. Trump, the least likely presidential candidate of all human history, was elected President of the United States. It sounds just as ridiculous to say it today as it felt ridiculous to *see* it then.

I, like so many other average Americans, snickered through the Republican debates, thinking to myself "Where in the *world* did they get these clowns?!" I watched with growing shock, dismay, and alarm as Trump knocked off every other (admittedly weak) GOP candidate, and then cruised effortlessly to the nomination.

While all this was frightening enough, the circus that followed was utterly surreal—disgraced former generals, shady international "businessmen," washed-up former conservative journalists, and every kind of ragtag sideshow personality you could name stepped forward to claim their place in the lurid spotlight. When the debates with Democratic nominee Hillary Clinton rolled around, each event was more bizarre than the next. Obvious untruths, half-truths, and outright lies poured forth from Trump's mouth like some kind of possessed PEZ dispenser. Hillary Clinton, widely viewed as our country's best hope for first woman president, was subjected to ridiculous taunts, misogynistic insinuations, outright personal insults, character assassinations, and just a massive barrage of utter bullshit that no one could possibly keep tabs on or make sense of. While Trump was a treasure trove of un-presidential behavior—brimming with past obscenities, indiscretions, business failures, and unseemly public behavior—each attempt to point out these obvious shortcomings fell on the totally deaf ears of his spookily enthralled followers.

At the final debate, Trump resorted to looming over her like some kind of twisted daddy-figure chaperone, making faces, speaking over her in childish outbursts, and mumbling to himself in a fashion that can only be described as reminiscent of an elderly dementia patient. Understandably, democratic viewers saw each debate as a rout, with Clinton being the only person in the room even *remotely* appearing able to represent the country—unless, of course, we were being represented at a tractor pull/mud-wrestling match. Most republican viewers were appalled as well, but a significantly large enough segment of them were so drawn in by this carnival barker of a human being that they, instead, saw just the opposite. Hillary, to them, was this crooked, conniving, secretive, otherworldly creature who had to be stopped from achieving power—and Trump was just the clear-eyed crusader for the job.

When the election grew nearer, no one with any normal understanding of politics could have fathomed the possibility that this human caricature of a sleazy used car salesman would ever receive a significant number of votes—let alone prevail and become president. It was unthinkable!

When the unbelievable came to pass, I was devastated. I couldn't see myself going on as the person I was before. Everything I thought I knew to be true about the world had turned out to be wrong, and I questioned how we would survive. The barbarians had climbed the wall, and Rome was coming apart at the seams. I knew that everyone I knew was just as shocked and mystified as I was, and if anyone was going to be able to calm me and get me through this historical episode, however long or brief, it was going to have to be . . .*ME*. I also felt like someone had to pick up the banner of courage and trudge forth into this new *bizarro* world and rally the troops as best he or she could. While I wasn't sure I personally was the best choice for this job, no one else seemed able to think or function any better at the moment and I was afraid if we waited around too long for someone to head up the care of the fallen, they might all just recede into the shadows and give up.

I started a blog, and since I couldn't claim any actual *qualifications* for rallying the sensible and struggling, I just called it "The Way I See It."

Each day, as news came in about the most recent assault on democracy, failure of decency, or just plain old act of criminality, I tried to identify exactly what was the significant pillar of civilization or ingredient of the resilient human spirit that had been trampled upon and addressed my post to that reality. Sometimes, I would find myself with a definite issue or virtue to tackle. At other times, I could only examine my emotions at the moment, imagine that others could be feeling the same way, and run verbally toward some distant speck of daylight to show that hope was not lost.

I found myself reaffirming my values, heard myself repeating the very best advice I'd ever been given, and re-awoke to consciousness reading pages I couldn't remember writing that were seemingly written by someone else. This person writing believed the same things I always claimed to, but could somehow present the issues and make responses to unfolding events in a much more cogent manner than I had ever been able to do. The election of Donald. J. "Big Orange" Trump had awakened my inner calm and given me a heightened capacity for introspection. And while I had not necessarily come to terms with the fate of our country (far from it, in fact), I *had* developed the ability to put aside my anger and dismay just long enough to cope with the overwhelming encroachment of dread we all felt.

This blog-now-book has been a salvation for me. It has buoyed me up when I was flagging, refocused me when I was discombobulated, and given me hope and faith that no matter how far down the road to oblivion this administration may collectively drags us, The United States of America has many better days ahead of it. We will all get through this catastrophe, and if we are careful, we may even learn something about ourselves in the process.

MONDAY, JANUARY 16TH, 2017 *was Martin Luther King Day. The reality of the upcoming inauguration was closing in on me and I stopped to think about how much MLK and his followers had to fear during the civil rights struggle and yet how they persevered and showed courage. They were walking into utter darkness in the social climate of the 1960s. It reminded me of how much they had gained for us all by protesting and insisting on what were basic human rights. While the territory Martin Luther King, Jr. trod was completely unknown, the task ahead of us is not. We know what needs to be done, because people have been there before and have shown us the way. This present political setback is no different. While the extreme nature of the rhetoric argues for counting this as new terrain, in truth, we've been here before.*

WALKING IN DARKNESS

I am amazed at my grownup self when I am alone at the cabin or go to the office to do work late at night. I have learned to walk in near total darkness, hands outstretched to find a familiar light switch or doorway, with no fear or dread whatsoever. When I was a child, I was plagued with little secret fears of what might be lurking in the dark. Ghost stories (which I loved), and horror movies (which I also loved) showed me a dizzying array of creatures that could be lurking just behind that door. When I heard noises in the night, I would lie in paralyzed fear that I was hearing the sticky creep of the creature from the black lagoon, or the rolling galumph of the blob coming to absorb me into its gelatinous bulk. Intellectually I knew there was no boogeyman, but in practice I had my doubts. Even in my own house, I was terrified of trekking into any room with no light on. Heart thumping, eyes wide, I would rush to the nearest light, turn it on, and quickly sweep the entire room with my eyes, certain I was about to see something horrific waiting to devour me in the darkest corner of the room.

Well, now I'm a grownup. I have a mental map of my office, my house, our cabin, the church office—all accurate enough that I don't need light to maneuver in those spaces. My knowledge of the world around me, coupled with my life experiences (of NOT finding a Chupacabra hiding anywhere in my house), have made it possible for me to dive into a darkened room and get right to what I need without fear.

Being afraid of the dark is a good metaphor for our fear of the unknown, our fear of the "other." We have been told that change is scary, that this or that type of person are out to get us, that certain ideas held by those we don't understand are unnatural or sinister. These ideas have been disproven, however, time and again and we have concrete experiences of meeting new people who turned out to be wonderful friends. We have quit jobs and tried new experiences and found them exhilarating and life-affirming. We have discussed wide-ranging topics with those who disagree with us and come away with a better understanding, and sometimes a slightly changed outlook. So, we know that what we have been told is untrue.

You have a reliable mental map of the world. You know what awaits you, the people who are waiting to befriend you, the energy you gain when you try something for the first time, the new understanding that is discoverable if you'll only seek it. But you don't step forward. You might fail. You might meet resistance. You might be done in by one of those "others."

You are not afraid of the dark. You have walked this path before and your intellect, as well as your rich experience tells you that everything is going to be alright. Step forward. Go in the direction of what you know is your path and defy the darkness.

"Darkness cannot drive out darkness, only light can do that. Hate cannot drive out hate, only love can do that." — Martin Luther King, Jr.

FRIDAY, JANUARY 20TH, 2017, *Donald J. Trump took the oath of office of President of the United States. It was a dull, wet, and cold day—exactly the way most people in the country felt about his election. While I found myself completely unable to think clearly, the thought that so many other people felt the same way made me commit to listening to others and trying to work out my despair through listening to theirs. This was my first blog post:*

DREARY, GRAY, RESTFUL

Driving in the gray rain, I find my mood darkening. It is cold and, for four days, when it was not pouring, it has drizzled. I listen to my mother chatter on about her daily troubles—not a complaint, but a litany of constant annoyances and trivial inconveniences. As I listen to her relate her saga, I find my own cares fade in prominence, not gone but seemingly further away, part of the wallpaper of my consciousness instead of the center of the frame. I begin to see myself facing the world my mother describes and I am able to offer commiseration, if not solutions to her travails back home.

I have heard numerous people say "O, So and so is calling and I just don't have the strength to listen to her troubles," as they continue obsessing about their own worries. It is a distinct irony that we cheat ourselves of personal relief by refusing to display empathy for others. Is that the secret? Is this some overlooked miracle?

There are great mysteries hidden in oft-repeated sayings and talismans. Things you have heard and yet never understood can sometimes divulge their meanings at the strangest times. Even verses we've long since dismissed because they seem like saccharine platitudes with no connection to our real suffering often have hidden origins in profound truths.

> Lord, make me an instrument of Thy peace;
> where there is hatred, let me sow love;
> where there is injury, pardon;
> where there is doubt, faith;
> where there is despair, hope;
> where there is darkness, light;
> and where there is sadness, joy.
>
> O Divine Master,
> grant that I may not so much seek
> to be consoled as to console;
> to be understood, as to understand;
> to be loved, as to love;
> for it is in giving that we receive,

it is in pardoning that we are pardoned,
and it is in dying that we are born to eternal
life.

Was it written by St. Francis? Probably not. But while it sounds like some great selfless wish of a sainted individual, it hides within its lines a very real truth—

"For it is in giving that we receive." And in listening that we are heard.

LATER, ON JANUARY 20TH, 2017, *President Trump issues Executive Order 13765, which scales back parts of the Affordable Care Act. He furthermore suspends an Obama administration cut to the Federal Housing Authority mortgage insurance premiums. This set of actions is a direct threat upon the health and safety of the most vulnerable in our society. I find myself thinking about the treachery of these moves and how many of the very people who voted for Trump will be hurt by these two actions. If this is how he treats his friends . . .*

WISHING YOU WELL

When a person embarks on a journey into the unknown, or attempts a great feat, or returns from something significant, the people who attend are often called "well-wishers." These onlookers and hangers-on are often not necessarily close associates of the honoree, but simply curious citizens who want to feel closer to someone who has become prominent. In the strict sense, these folks may very well not "wish him or her well," per se, but they have shown up to watch. The term "well-wisher" is then, nothing more than a euphemism.

This is a trend in our society, to describe people and actions in convenient, if not accurate terms. People we went to school with were called our "classmates" —even though we had little in common and may well not have even known each other. People who connect with us on Facebook are our "friends," though they may be dropped and "unfriended" or at the very least "unfollowed" for very little cause.

Well, I am seceding from such traditions. I need my relationships to mean more—or at least as much as the term implies. This may seem trivial to some, but it is a beginning. A beginning of a personal move to seek meaning in my daily life. If I call you my friend, I want that to mean that I have a personal connection to you, that I condone and affirm intimate aspects of your character, that I would inconvenience myself in some way to help you if you found yourself in need. I would be a friend to you.

There are a small group of individuals whose personal characteristics cause me to admire and respect them. I find in these people a kinship and a comfort for the better parts of myself. I call these people friends. For the rest, I am, at least a well-wisher. But if I wish you well, I want to mean it.

I wish you well, and given the chance, I would hope that I would take actual measures to make your life better, to make you well. This we all need, friends of a small number, but well-wishers of all kinds. There are people out there who need to be made well— they are sick or hurt and need more than wishes. There are people who need food. There are people who need shelter. There are people who need medical care and health insurance. Wishes are not going to get this done. They need their friends, and absent that possibility, they need true well-wishers—the active kind. I challenge you to be just that. A true friend to the faithful few, and a well-wisher to mankind. Get to work.

SATURDAY, JANUARY 21, 2017, *four million people from all over the world attend the Women's March on Washington, D. C. Watching these determined and peaceful protesters trudge through the streets of our nation's capitol gives me a sense of solidarity with a larger "force" of humanity and spurs me to get my thoughts in order to be able to face what is ahead—whatever that might turn out to be—and to return to my meditation practice in order to calm the dread inside me.*

LONG TERM GOALS

It's always nice to have something to look forward to, isn't it? Though I often wonder if we aren't living for a future when the present is not so bad.

If a person we're sitting in prison, that'd be a great reason to look ahead. You'd live for the day you got out, right? But our present conditions are not all something we need to escape from or put out of our minds. There are things worth living through now and being fully conscious to enjoy them.

This is why the concept of mindfulness is so important. We've taught ourselves, when anything is challenging, or even just less than thrilling, to look through the present to some glad time when we'll be free of this drudgery. And this coping mechanism has its place— like in the first example, say prison. But we have learned this technique too well and many of us are future-huffing zombies with no appreciation for the NOW.

When you're on a vacation, you want to be in the now. When you're with the one you love, you savor every moment. But daily life needs to be savored too. A warm bath, a cup of coffee, a great smelling candle and a good book—these are little treats to bring our awareness back to the present and to help us live a little of this very day.

Meditation is a great tool to help us see the importance of living in THIS day, in THIS moment, in THIS life. Set aside time to relax and listen to your breath. Hear the inhaled breath, feel the exhaled breath. Concentrate only on the sensation of breathing. When outside sensations arise, notice, then return. If you find your thoughts wandering, say to yourself "inhale. . . exhale" as you breathe. Start with 10 minutes, and then go for 20 after you've been successful at that several times. You'll find, eventually, that you are able to look at life up close without diverting your mental focus to some happier future spot—and just maybe we'll find that the present can be enjoyed better than it can avoided.

Make living this moment a long-term goal.

I WAS ONE OF THE *people who said "Well, let's give the schmuck a chance. He certainly sounded like the worst possible candidate for this office, but maybe he'll grow out of it. That, as we now know, did not happen. A lot of the people, in any situation, who erupt into action right out of the gate are later proven to be too hasty by half. Others, with the same reaction in a different situation, are later vindicated by the realization that things truly are as bad as we thought.*

GIVE IT SOME TIME

I used to have trouble getting out of bed. I would wake up, usually to an alarm, feel terrible, and think "I just can't face this." Now, if I went back to sleep, I'd wake up again later and feel just as bad or maybe worse. However, if I got up, had a cup of coffee, relaxed watching the news or listening to music, *then* I'd start to feel human and realize I could face the day. I had to exert some energy to get up, do something to help myself (coffee), and then give it some time to take effect. Waiting a while before judging my day or my feelings always seemed to help.

A TRUMP DIARY

We are, by nature, reactionary. Our evolutionary tendencies are to follow our first instinct. Afraid? Run. Nervous? Distrust. Threatened? Attack! Surprised? Fear!

Now, there are times (like in a dark alley) when these ingrained tendencies are still appropriate, but for the most part, life is a bit more complicated than hiding in caves and watching for predators. (Although the political landscape is still existentially treacherous) Nowadays, if we run, we leave behind an opportunity we didn't see because we fled so precipitously. Fear plays a role but should be tempered with a wait and see attitude.

The masses of people who marched the day after the election are making a statement. While some think they are being reactionary, I think they are rather being cautious. By this I mean, they are not holing up in a bunker for fear of the onslaught. They are not booking a ticket to Finland (though some are tempted, I'm sure). They are not stockpiling supplies to survive the dystopian future (which may still come). Instead, they are making the calculated move to say "Things could get bad, but let's tell them what we care about first, and show them how many of us there are, and see if that tempers the pace of the about-face that appears to be in the works. Make a statement and give it a while.

Much like my morning rituals, they've gotten up, done something to help themselves, and now. . . We give it some time.

TRUMP *is obsessed with Twitter. He tweets morning, noon, and night. His worst, most inadvisable tweets sometimes come just before bedtime or upon first arising in the morning— sometimes as late as 3 am—as though he never slept at all. I think about the amount of time we all waste on our phones. I consider the unnatural amount of scrutiny we put others through on Facebook, Twitter, and Instagram. It occurs to me how unrealistic our interactions are becoming due to cell phones and the culture of the constantly jacked-in.*

OVERTHINKING IT

I haven't seen Alice in at least a week. Have you heard from her? I think she's mad at me—we usually speak every couple of days, so when she doesn't call, I just know I've done something to upset her. . . Really?!

When we haven't seen or heard from someone in a while, there are two distinct personal reactions. The first is from the novice mind. The Novice assumes the worst: our friend is dead, in trouble, angry, or up to something. There are no foreseeable circumstances where we don't know what's happening with someone that can be anything less than negative—maybe even catastrophic! The Novice (a term of my own here) is ruled by what Zen practitioners call "Monkey mind." This part of the psyche is never still, always thinking, always reaching, explaining —and in the absence of any actual information, making things up out of thin air.

Our present-day society has spoiled us with constant stimulation, constant communication, positively no "down time." We come to expect a constant stream of information at our fingertips. And in this atmosphere of over stimulation, it becomes practically unthinkable that we don't know what our friends are up to at any (or every) given moment. This explains why so many young people are glued to their phone and cannot seem to carry on a conversation, eat a meal, watch a tv show or movie, or sit for more than couple minutes without obsessively checking their email or social media updates. There is no world in which this can be sustained and not lead to psychosis. We must, MUST, learn for ourselves and our children to PUT DOWN THE PHONE. Our excessive phone-i-ness has stunted our ability to think clearly, hold a conversation, pursue a problem, or just to be present for another human being when they need us. It is unsustainable, crass, and inhuman.

The second reaction to the absence of a friend from our sight and hearing is that of the Adept (my term also). The Adept, while likely still struggling with monkey mind, has accepted that we cannot know everything all the time. People can exist out of our sphere of knowledge and not be either in peril or upset with us. They will call eventually. Of course, if you don't hear from your friend in a timely manner, a polite email or phone call to say "hadn't heard from you and just wondered how you were" is certainly appropriate and often appreciated. The truth is, time away from a friend is often constructive to both parties. "Absence makes the heart grow fonder." Also "no news is good news" comes to mind.

Aspects of both the Adept and the Novice mind exist side by side in our consciousness. The mindset that dominates is the one you feed. Refuse to assume, meditate in order not to obsess, spend time alone, spend focused one-on-one time with your friends and family, and PUT DOWN THE PHONE.

It is time to establish 21st century etiquette—not because we can't get by without it, but because we are less human without it. Our spirits cry out for liberation from this tyranny of electronic "minders." Setting boundaries will ennoble our personal interactions and help us to feed the mind of calm, clear vision.

Suggestions:

1. No phones in Restaurants or meals (none)
2. No phones in bed
3. No phones when watching tv or movies
4. No phones in meetings (ever—EVER)
5. No phones on vacations (except during down time, or at the end of the day when you are alone)

6. No phones while driving DUH
7. No phones while doing your job (unless it IS your job)

This is all for our own good—and while I will struggle to uphold this set of rules just like you, I believe this is truly a necessary step.

MONDAY, JANUARY 23RD, 2017, *President Trump signs three memoranda: 1. Withdrawing the United States from the Trans-Pacific Partnership, 2. Reinstating the "Mexico City Policy," barring international NGOs from receiving U.S. funding if they "offer or promote abortions as part of their family planning services," and 3. Initiating a 90-day hiring freeze on the federal workforce. Later that day, a lawsuit is filed in federal court, accusing Trump of violating the emoluments clause of the constitution. It makes me think that we are beginning to withdraw ourselves from the world scene and abdicate our responsibilities to change the world for the better.*

BUILDING A WORLD

One of the primary founders of our country, Thomas Jefferson, spent the majority of his adult life building a house. Well, he spent part of it building, part tearing it down, and then rebuilding. Monticello, a glorious, classically inspired mansion on a mini mountain in Charlottesville Virginia, is a story in brick, wood, stone, and glass. It is the story of the aspirations and experiments of an extraordinary enlightenment thinker and democratic social architect. As Jefferson more clearly realized his grand plan for his personal residence, he tore down parts of his home and replaced it with vastly different elements. The end result, which was never fully finished in his lifetime, is a masterpiece to behold and logs more visitors than any historical monument outside of Washington, DC.

We are building a world. Every day. Every action and thought either placing a brick in the edifice or taking one down. Our deeds and words are bricks, our thoughts the cement that holds them together.

Each of us, throughout our days, has built up a great city of acts and expression. We have, many times, also torn it back down and had to start over. Sometimes we caught ourselves halfway and were able to salvage the remaining structure and simply repair it. But other times, friendships and constructive relationships were totally disassembled and had to be either recreated or abandoned.

We build our world through how we choose to relate to our fellow human beings, how we support or refuse to support justice and kindness, and whether we are passing on our wisdom, goodwill, and resources. John Donne said, "No man is an island," and it's still true—the fate of others affects us whether we want to acknowledge it or not. Those who look at others as interlopers or competitors are trying to isolate their own progress from that of their fellow man. This cannot, in fact, be done. It is an illusion.

When any one area or subgroup is poorer, less educated, or downtrodden, we are all the worse off for it. The social unrest, economic stagnation, global morale, and net inequality affect our lives and the lives of the generations we leave behind when we die and bequeath this world to the next generation. When the air is dirtier, the resources scarcer, the water less potable, the populace less empowered, we are creating a future of human misery—and some people believe we will be held accountable for it in a cosmic, eternal result.

What can I do? How can I build this world positively? How can I be the solution instead of the problem?

Support young people, advocate for quality education that is delivered without consideration of economic condition, speak out against injustice, give time and resources to positive organizations that do good work, resist people and ideas that divide us into good people and "others," listen to people who disagree and only after really listening, try to win them to these principles, give things away as a part of your daily life, stop collecting pointless possessions, invest in goodness. And think good thoughts . . . to hold your efforts together.

XENOPHOBIA *is a term that keeps raising its ugly head—and rightfully so. It is truly amazing that such a large group of people who claim, on the whole, to be Christian in their religion, can be so easily led to abandon the primary tenet of that religion. Hospitality. The Old Testament screams it, through the story of Sodom and Gomorrah. The New Testament bases the whole of our proof of belief in Jesus and his teaching on stories like the "Good Samaritan." But here we stand, listening to so-called Christians talk about turning away those "dirty foreigners." It is further distressing that the only country on earth with no true ethnic history except for that of immigrants is being turned against the very peoples who built our country from nothing.*

WELCOMING STRANGERS

When were you a stranger? New to the environs? First day on the job? Immigrant? Displaced by tragedy? Who welcomed you? How much did it mean at the time?

We encounter people every day who are out of sorts—new to the area, fresh out of a relationship, newbie in a group or club, visiting our church or social club, or just wandered into an unfamiliar area of town. Our first instinct is to say "Hi, my name is X, and I was wondering if you needed someone to show you around?" Why is that? Because we've been there.

Do you remember the people in middle school and high school who ran as a clique and wouldn't let you sit at their lunch table? The neighborhood bully who needed to intimidate someone new everyday just to feel good about himself? The enforcers of choosing teams who made sure you were chosen last or not chosen at all? The people who recognized you as unfamiliar and turned their backs or locked their car doors? The ones who covered their mouths and whispered to people near them as if to say, "that's not one of US!"

Do you remember the kind souls who approached you when you were new and introduced themselves? Who let you eat with their friends and introduced you around to other friends? Who brought you a little gift to welcome you to the neighborhood? Who sponsored you so you could join a club or community group? Invited to their church and made you feel like you belonged? Yes, we remember those people too.

Which of these two types do you want to emulate? Which of the ways you were made to feel do you want to pass on to as many people as possible? That's what I thought. . .

We are not called to love only those whom we know, not to be kind to only those who look like us, talk like us, worship like us— but everyone. If this seems like a self-evident truth to you, then the most recent political moves we're seeing banning people from certain countries and favoring one religion over another will shine for what they are, anathema to the spirit of our great country.

This is not a political book. It is a book about life, growing, learning, aging, reflecting, and interacting with our inner thoughts and the inner thoughts and feelings of others. But, you see, here is where the two streams of experience intersect. This is furthermore not a religious book, and yet there is no better way to say it:

Then shall he say also unto them on the left hand, "Depart from me, ye cursed, into everlasting fire, prepared for the devil and his angels: For I was hungered, and ye gave me no meat: I was thirsty, and ye gave me no drink: I was a stranger, and ye took me not in: naked, and ye clothed me not: sick, and in prison, and ye visited me not." Then shall they also answer him, saying, "Lord, when saw we thee hungered, or athirst, or a stranger, or naked, or sick, or in prison, and did not minister unto thee?" Then shall he answer them, saying, "Verily I say unto you, inasmuch as ye did it not to one of the least of these, ye did it not to me." — (KJV) St. Matthew 25

The witness may step down.

TRUMP USES PUBLIC INSULTS *to bludgeon his enemies into silence and to ridicule those who call out his obvious and fatal flaws. You don't need to witness it more than once to begin to feel slimy—like you've just watched your grandma pee off the front porch. There is something decidedly disheartening and demoralizing watching the (once) leader of the free world engage in behavior we discourage in middle school students. His public taunts have run the gamut from celebrities (Rosie O'Donnell), to sports figures (Colin Kaepernick), to other politicians ("Crooked" Hillary, "Little" Marco Rubio, and "Boring" Jeb Bush come to mind.) No amount of criticism can dissuade him from continuing the embarrassing practice. After one particularly frustrating day of watching him degrade the office of president, I wrote this:*

SAVE THE SNARK

It doesn't happen just in professional circles, but it's at its worst there. The snark. You do your interior work, you strive to be a good person, you suppress every urge to correct people, you strive to want the best for EVERYONE. And then it happens. Some poor idiot who, please forgive my candor, couldn't find his butt with both hands. . . comes for you. No provocation, no obvious personal gain to be seen, but they see the opportunity and they unload the snark.

The old you would have ruined them, after all, you obviously have the skills— and here is a poor clown not worthy to unclasp your snark sandals. Their facts are thin, their delivery was amateur, the shot was so obvious and so cheap that no one would fault you. . . But you pause to reflect. This is a sign of great progress. Control is the key to all progress.

But why? Why not just pursue the scorched earth policy perfected in your youth? It. Would. Be. So. Easy. . .

No. It's not worth the kind of psychic connection to old habits that could drag you down in other ways. You are now dealing with bigger fish— and you're looking forward to whales.

The work of tearing people down is important, but only to the ones being torn down—their humiliation is a trigger to spur their personal growth. You've been there, made use of the opportunity, and are now on a better path. This path is leading somewhere, it's working, its benefits are tangible, palpable, spiritually nourishing, and there is no turning back. The momentary joy of squashing someone who desperately needs squashing is a fleeting victory— not the kind of lasting emotional accomplishment that moves you closer to the goal. And once territory has been traversed, the truest path does not lead past that spot again— relearning is anticlimactic, and a bitter reminder of incremental failure.

You respond tactfully, barely cognizant of the slight, and move on with your life. Not today, poor novice— you'll have to bait someone less evolved to get your lesson, but make no mistake, it's coming, and you do deserve it.

Will a day come when you take the bait? Will your control falter eventually? Will you ultimately be drawn into the dance of the unevolved again and have to bear the shame of recidivism?

Maybe. But not today.

BEING THIN-SKINNED *is perhaps one of Trump's worst character traits. He feels insulted by the mere act of someone disagreeing with him—it's really kind of astonishing. He considers any criticism of him to be a criticism of his very being—and any criticism of his government's policies as an insult to the country. Trump's self-worth is wrapped up in his materialism. When he brags, it's nearly always about his (supposed) accomplishments. Wealth, fame, possessions, and good press are the only things that seem to calm his angst at the condition of the world and its attitude toward him. You could count friends and family among those things that give him comfort, but he doesn't really have any lasting friends. He was once "friends" with Bill and Hillary Clinton—two people he now denigrates ad nauseum. He was once "friends" with Megan Kelly, but a few simple comments on his behavior and she became a punching bag for his misogyny. Recognizing this made me thankful for all the things and people in my life that I am thankful for.*

TRUE BLESSINGS

What do you consider a blessing? Money? Position? Adventure? Ease? These things are advantageous, and certainly to be desired—but what are your real blessings? For me, it is people. Old friends, new friends, and fellow strivers in music.

For others, it might be time to pray, or gathered family, or opportunities to taste really fine food— it doesn't matter what the content of your true earthly treasures might be, it matters that you know what they are, appreciate them, and guard them from becoming just another "thing."

Secondary in importance to good people, I enjoy travel and authentic food. Somewhere in the mix, I am thankful for solitude, good books to read, and the ability to create through both physical building and musical composition. But all of this must take a backseat to people.

Is there really any better feeling than sharing ideas with good people? Is there any more satisfying experience than sharing a laugh with another intelligent person? Conversation, shared experience, intellectual interaction, and just plain old *bonhomie*— this is my heaven on earth.

Because I love people, I eschew formality. I try to be plain spoken, that is, I say what I mean — it is important to me that friends know I mean what I say and that I am not out to trick or use anyone. The world seems to be filled with insincere and manipulative people. They say anything it takes to convince the world they mean one thing, while in reality they have kept their whole mind set upon another thing entirely and lead those around them circuitously in order to achieve that secret goal. I have many former friends who fall into that category— it's not that I've completely forsaken their friendship, but since their constant subterfuge is so obvious, I cannot bring myself to trust them anymore. Trust is important. Without it, we are awash in lonely landscape of dog-eat-dog daily living, which is tiresome and demoralizing.

There was an old gospel song my grandmother loved called "Count your blessings." The composer was Edwin Excel:

When upon life's billows you are tempest-tossed
When you are discouraged, thinking all is lost,
Count your many blessings, name them one by one
And it will surprise you what the Lord has done!

The rest is really repetitive, but the message is clear and useful— do not dwell on the challenges facing you, do not allow the adversity of the present moment to blind you to the strength of your advantages. And whether God, or Providence, or happenstance, or the nurturing and infinite universe is handing you blessings, RECOGNIZE them, ACKNOWLEDGE them, be THANKFUL for them, and NEVER FORGET that they offer you comfort and a wellspring of support that should never be forgotten.

Count your blessings. Name them, claim them, thank them, and do all you can to keep them around. Then try to be a blessing to someone else. THAT is the appropriate response every time.

Thank you to my blessings!

THE DAILY ONSLAUGHT *of Trump's crassness and ignorance can be distressing. Cable news and Facebook only compound the problem. I needed a vacation, and I took one— both from work, and from the news.*

CHANGE OF SCENERY

Never should we underestimate the power of time away. It is not the case that the alternate destination to which we repair must be exotic, although exotic locales have their charm. It is not necessary for the retreat to be a distant hideaway, inaccessible by the masses, although such places are exciting. There is, likewise, no requirement that the vacation be taken somewhere expensive— spending large sums of cash can bring its own worries and work against the desired effect of time away.

No, the location, length of stay, cost of lodgings, distance from home, nor any mundane measure of the respite can be shown to be the true magic behind a person's need for retreat— the actual effect comes from breaking our daily patterns and changing our typical vistas.

It has been said that the definition of insanity is "doing the same thing over again and expecting different results." This is indeed a crazy endeavor. For scientific research basically proves that the more variables remain the same from experiment to experiment, the more likely that the outcome will not change. If your daily routine causes you boredom today, it will, likewise, cause you boredom three weeks from now— perhaps even more intensely so due to the compounding effect of repetition. You can indeed PERFECT boredom.

Humans need to break the pattern, to change the wallpaper, to freshen the breeze, to toss it all out and start over. I remember a well-meaning friend saying to me when I was contemplating leaving one job and starting another, "You know, there's going to be shit at this new job, too—right?" I replied, "Yes, I know that— but it'll be DIFFERENT shit!"

I am so amazingly refreshed upon returning from vacation. I am not saying all my problems are solved—hardly— but they weigh on me so much less heavily simply because I've had time away from DWELLLING on them. I can see things from a different perspective—and whether or not this new angle causes a breakthrough or not really doesn't matter. The change in outlook is enough. The refreshing proof that somewhere, somehow, someday, my problems are completely irrelevant and do not cloud the view of my life is such a great comfort to me.

On my return journey, we listened to a book on FDR. Franklin Roosevelt, admittedly, had very little experience in finance. He had nearly zero executive experience or inclination before winning governor of New York. But his life experiences made him look at things differently— radically differently. He was an active, boisterous, strapping young man until contracting polio. The change he witnessed in the way people related to him after he became disabled made him want desperately to regain the normalcy he had felt before the disease racked his lower extremities. His sunny, often irrational exuberance was the affect he found necessary to get people to stop seeing him as a "poor cripple" and to begin to follow his leadership. The CHANGE in outlook that FDR experienced from his changed world of ill health empowered him to change others' opinion of him and to get them to change their behavior— this ability won him not only the governorship of New York, but multiple terms as US President. His leadership saved the US economy from the clutches of the depression and despair and aided in winning WWII. A change of perspective did all that—a drastic change admittedly— but nonetheless a simple change in perspective was unendingly POWERFUL!

When the collapse of the economy was at its worst, Herbert Hoover insisted that nothing should change — not the banks, not the monetary standard, not a single thing. He would simply wait this downturn out and it would wither and die in the face of normalcy. FDR's change of perspective showed the need for change —lots of it— but the biggest change of all was just in attitude. The sunny outlook and can-do attitude of Franklin Roosevelt convinced Americans that happy days were definitely on their way (if not exactly "here again"). His ability to see a way forward came from his being forced to look at things differently— and we must learn from the example.

We may not need to save a national economy, or win a world war, but the troubles we do face will always benefit from our allowing ourselves time away, changed perspective, and the benefit of an attitude adjustment.

WHO IS THIS GUY? *We find ourselves asking this on a regular basis. But the real question that needs asking is not "who is he?" The important question is "Who are WE?" When we forget who we are, when we forget that we are the indispensable nation. When we allow ourselves to cease seeing ourselves as the "shining city on a hill," of the Old Testament writer's allusion, we are giving the pernicious elements in this fight a decided advantage. Before we size up the enemy, let's think about who we are and what we are fighting for. It is absolutely essential to winning the fight.*

REMEMBERING SELF

I was so discouraged. I was at my wit's end, alienated from my values, annoyed to the point of distraction by people to whom I would normally pay no mind. I couldn't think straight—all I could think of was how these folks annoyed and demoralizing me. Why was I so STUCK?

Well, I eventually figured out I had lost focus on my identity— I had forgotten WHO I was, I had lost my hold on the centering idea of SELF. The person I was—my true self would NEVER let people with so little intelligence and self-awareness get me down. How could I let this happen? Well, in this world of viciously competing ideals and morals, it is easy to become drawn into the arguments and struggles that divide people instead of remembering the things that we hold in common and that give us a reason to rally to each other's defense. It is often just a small step to one side from being incensed by an unjust world to being thrown into confusion by the onslaught of competing ideas.

Well, who AM I? I am my mother's son—my mother who is a force of nature, undaunted, unafraid, uncensored, unleashed, and fearsome to behold. I am the son of Joyce— who directs the lives of anyone who needs it, or anyone who cannot direct themselves, or even just someone who stands around a moment too long in inaction. The strong, the sure, the fierce, the unstoppable. Who gives until someone stops her, and even then is not happy to stop—because who else is going to do it?

I am my father's son—my father who labored harder than anyone who ever worked for him, who was never too good for anyone and laughed at anyone who was, who was the fairest and most honest man who ever ran a farm or anything else. Stubborn, proud, strong Sonny— industrious, and long suffering, and able to laugh at himself and everyone else when necessary.

I am my grandmothers' grandson— both of them! Ruth, righteous and prayerful, faithful to her beliefs and values throughout a life full of hardships and disappointments. A beacon of faith and fortitude to everyone who knew her, an inspiration. Geneva, joyful and irreverent, singing to herself through her daily work—collecting and remembering stories from the past, laughing at the folly of prideful relatives and neighbors because she recognized the equality of us all, dying young of cancer from an asbestos infested homestead yet an unbreakable spirit to the end!

I have earned my abilities and scars— worked hard on the farm and pushed myself to learn music on my own, first church job at 14, first house at 21, teaching college level at 23, traveled the world extensively and convinced it's the secret to life! I believe in equality, industry, kindness, perseverance, forgiveness, renewal, redemption, tolerance, education, reinvention, mentorship, gratitude, and love. And I believe that all the misguided evil that plagues us at this moment will fall beneath the crush of resurgent intelligence and goodwill that may be in a waning state now, but will wax again strong, refreshing, and resplendent in a new day that even now is girding itself for eternal victory! I'm remembering myself. That's who I am.

Who are you? When will you allow yourself to remember? Are you clinging to false friends, a dead relationship, a hateful religion, a job you've long since grown beyond, resentment that sours your soul, addiction that robs you of joy, stagnation that is killing you by degrees? Let go, return to yourself, leave the false trappings behind. You may be someone you've not yet even met—don't you want to?

It's time. . .

THE TAX BILL *Republicans passed was a love letter to corporations and the wealthy. The giveaway was staggering! Over $1.5 TRILLION in tax cuts and code changes that benefit them. Trump supporters seemed oblivious to the fact that their own tax breaks in this bill (Such as they are) were set to expire in a few years, but the cuts for corporations and millionaires . . . well, of course, they go on forever.*

SELF-INTEREST

We've got have enough to keep ourselves warm and dry, prepare for the future, and not to be taken advantage of in business. But – and this is a big but— too much self-interest is known as greed and is the greatest sin in America today.

We hear a lot of people carping loudly about THEIR TAXES. Too high. About THEIR TAXES going to lazy people who don't work — well, there are few problems with these folks. First, they can't count. If you break down what everyone in America pays in taxes, you will find out that the average American pay is $1.46 per paycheck to help other people. $1.46. Everything else, and there is a lot that goes to their own Social Security, their own Medicare, their own retirement savings, and to pay for roads, sewers, and all the things that every municipality needs and that we all share. The problem is, these folks are either not curious enough to investigate, or not smart enough to figure it out when they do – and somehow, they think that some huge portion of their taxes is going to help "lazy people." Secondly, the same people these tax-averse folks are voting for, are the ones who spend billions – yes, I said billions, of our government money on wars and the military-industrial complex. This money, aside from funding a lot of jobs that we all may care about, does not go to "lazy people." However, if you are just gullible enough to listen to the people selling this theory, and just lazy enough to not want to investigate for yourself, you might be fooled into thinking there is no distinction between these two piles of money.

The Republican healthcare plan is one huge screw job on the American public. It takes away protections the ACA gave us, it's strips away subsidies that help people to pay for insurance, it cancels the requirement that everyone buy health insurance (which was the only reason the rates could ever become affordable.), and it gives away billions, yes, billions to millionaires and billionaires and to the healthcare industry. Protections for people with pre-existing conditions are wiped away. Protections for older people to keep them from being charged huge surcharges for being old are wiped away. Protections for women, protections for those with mental illnesses, protections for children, protections for anyone who might either get sick or get old are all wiped away.

This bill is mean. This bill is regressive. This bill is vindictive. This bill is sloppy. This bill was written by people who were paid to write it, to suit their masters – the insurance industry and the wealthy.

STOP THIS BILL. We are better than this, and we need to stand up and tell the Republicans that we are not going to let them get away with hurting 27 million people. That is how many people will be thrown off the insurance rolls if this bill is enacted. Get informed, get active, and get this bill defeated.

GRATITUDE IS THE KEY. *It is the only thing I have found that can lift my spirits regardless of what Trump is doing at the moment. The mere recognition that I still have innumerable gifts to be thankful for can quickly take me from the depths of despair (where did this IDIOT come from?), to a place of relative peace (he can't last forever). Many people have it rough. Maybe that's why progressives like myself are so perturbed with this selfish and malevolent regime, because we understand just how many people live on the brink of financial collapse every day. And the time we spend dilly-dallying about with this fake president could be spent working for a "more perfect union."*

GRATITUDE CHECK

Are you paying attention? Have you noticed? Do you recognize how good you've got it? Allow me to assist you. . . Do you have clean water? Parts of Appalachia would appreciate it if you didn't take that for granted. Many places in Africa would do anything to be in your spot. Do you have decent clothing and a way to wash them? Clothes closets for the needy are booming—why? Drop by and ask them. Is your house cool/warm enough and can you afford to keep it that way? You can donate to those who struggle with this on your electric and gas bills— if you've neglected to be thankful for this luxury, perhaps that's your next step.

Food? Enough? Variety? Can you cook in your house because you have more than adequate groceries? Inner cities have huge "food deserts" where only convenience goods and 3rd rate produce are available. Can you grow a garden like me? Pray tonight, really hard, and thank God for your good fortune—then share the bounty when it comes. It's only fair. How's your job? Are you secure in it? Do you like what you do? Is there a future for you in this field? Do you have colleagues you like, trust, and enjoy? Don't let the unemployment numbers fool you, MANY people are in jobs that are either stressful to the point of unhealthiness, or insecure, or unpleasant due to environment or workload, or pay next to nothing, or are ruled by cruel, screaming idiots. Help someone else get or prepare to get a good job. It's only right.

Does somebody love you? Family? Friends? A significant other? MORE than one person?!? Wow, you are so lucky! You are just the golden ticket winner in life—and were you aware? No?! Really?! This is bad, you need to wake up! Find the people who love you today, thank them. Tell them how much they mean to you, cherish them. Do it now!

This is not a dress rehearsal. This is not an accident of chance that you have what you have. The universe has bestowed upon you blessings that cannot be overestimated in their worth. You are a truly fortunate individual and you need to start living like it's true! One moment, one day, one instant—and it can all be gone. Is that really when you want to realize what you have? When you no longer have it? Really?!? No. I didn't think so.

Do others have more than you? Of course, they do! It's just logical that there will be those with more—but who really needs more than what should be making you deliriously happy RIGHT NOW? Are you thankful? Time to prove it—volunteer today, donate now, go out and help someone, be a friend, say a prayer, offer to assist, give away what you don't need, invite someone over for dinner, tell someone you love them.

Gratitude check. . .

PREVIOUS PRESIDENTS *of the United States have dedicated herculean amounts of time to their jobs—early mornings (George W. Bush was up at the crack of dawn), late nights (President Obama had meetings at midnight when things got harried), and very few actual breaks for recreation and unwinding. President Reagan and George W. Bush got no small amount of criticism for the number of "vacation days" they spent at their respective "Western White Houses." But no president or any other head of state has even approached the level of sloth that Trump has exhibited. Work days that begin at 11:00 am, bedtimes as early as 6:30 pm, and huge swaths of what his staff has labeled "Executive Time," where he basically watches television and tweets out inane pronouncements that wreak havoc on the attempts of congress to create any illusion of business as usual. In the midst of all this "non-work," he has visited more golf courses than Arnold Palmer and seems to have no qualms about simply pissing away the people's time while he is charged with doing their government's business. No, this chief executive just doesn't have any sense of a work ethic, or of the importance of diligently attending to national and international crises. Puerto Rico languished without power for months, and the president hardly mentioned the embattled*

island after the initial hurricane emergency had been addressed.
I wondered about where one gets a "work ethic."

HARD WORK

When I was a kid, I hated hard work. I dreaded it, resented it, hid from it, moaned and groaned about it. I felt specially singled out for punishment by God to have been placed on a farm and to have been subjected to daily, rigorous labor. But, because of being made to work daily and to accept hard labor as part of what life is about. I learned a few things.

The effects of learning to work hard:

1. The ability to make long range-plans—I can see what a project will look like waaaay down the road because of being involved in jobs that took month-long stretches of work. When I look at a project that is going to take a long time to finish, instead of being put off or despairing of the work to come, I start seeing the steps that will be needed to bring the work to a conclusion.
2. The ability to settle into unpleasant work (physical or mental) for the long haul. I am steadfast and undaunted.
3. The ability to be analytical. I can estimate what a multi-level endeavor will cost and whether it's worth paying for or should just be done myself.
4. Faith in your own abilities. There have been enough tough spots in my past, casting doubt on whether I

had what it took—but I came through— and now it's clear what my skills are.

5. Strong muscles that take very little re-engagement to spring back to life and help one finish hard tasks.

6. People ask my opinion on their projects —and I feel capable of offering advice.

7. A low tolerance for laziness. When young people show that they are lazy, I think badly. . . of their parents. I see the job of building strength and character as belonging to parents.

8. The ability to recover quickly—from physical fatigue as well as mental stress.

9. The capacity for being emotionally renewed by physical labor. Even as I age, and BOY HOWDY do I feel the effects of aging, I need frequent physical activity to thrive. Strangely, mindless exercise doesn't appeal to me at all— I need an end result to the work — a final state of accomplishment.

Because I have benefited so fully from learning hard work and all it does for one's body and character, I believe in its use with young people.

Try it. Insist that your children have jobs in the household— real responsibility. Cleaning the dishes after dinner is a good start, but mowing the yard, taking out the trash, cleaning up after animals, putting away groceries, decorating for holidays and taking down those decorations afterwards—all this and more are very simple things that even the smallest kids can and *should* be required to do. Will they be thrilled about it? No. But the lessons and respect for work that they learn through these simple, banal activities will change them for the better. Make this a priority in your child-rearing plan. You'll be glad you did—and your kids will thank you (not right away) but later.

ONE OF THE MOST DISTURBING TRENDS
*brought about (or at least exacerbated by) the Trump ascendancy
has been the insinuation of cheap litmus-test-like qualifications
into the discussion of what it means to be an American, or
a patriotic American at least. Loving our country has been
equated with insisting on "America first" policies, suspicion
of anyone from another country, a steroid-injected sensibility
toward the military and insistence on its sacredness, and a
number of truly trivial notions of what constitutes deference
toward our republic and its history. The same people who
claim to be such great patriots and denigrate those they see
as not exhibiting acceptable levels of public fealty to our flag,
or military, or the president (This president—it was fine to
denigrate the last one—he wasn't real) can be found giving
ridiculously intricate and fabricated excuses for the lapses of this
president that most Americans consider un-American. Donald
Trump has most assuredly violated the emoluments clause of
the constitution, and profits from foreign investments daily—
not to mention how he profits from the Secret Service and
government functionaries having to follow him from Trump
property to Trump property, and having the government pay
for their lodging and upkeep to his personally owned businesses.*

These activities do not faze Trump supporters even a smidgeon. Trump also hired a baker's dozen of questionable characters into his administration—some in the most sensitive positions—who have all now, slowly, begun to be discovered as criminals, or at least as shady, under-qualified hacks! Are super patriots bothered by any of this? No! Anybody can make a few mistakes in hiring bad people. (Never mind, we were supposedly sold on this windbag because he would "hire the best people," and make the "best deals.") Well, how do we celebrate America in a way that helps us get through this sad state of reality?

DECLARING INDEPENDENCE

We are all aware of the story of American Independence—the grievances, the distrust, the disrespect of a distant monarch, and the final break with mother England. Colonists were tired of taxes they had no say in, governors they couldn't un-elect, roads they couldn't request finances to build, court cases decided by foreigners, and much more. The founding parents were declaring independence from many things — and from time to time, we must do the same. Here are a few suggestions.

- Declare yourself independent from bitterness. Accept past wrongs, forgive them, and move on with your life!

- Declare your independence from jealousy. Be happy when good things happen to others and recognize your own blessings.

- Declare an end to judgmentalism. Let people live—are they perfect? No. Are they just what you want or wish them to be? No. That's life. Get over it.

- Separate yourself from ego. What?! Yes, ego. It only makes you look silly. Yes, everyone has a measure of difficulty with this, but it's common and it makes YOU look common. Rise ABOVE. You want folks to think you're great? Stop showing them that YOU ALREADY THINK THAT. It really is the saddest and most comical human foible.

- Declare a holiday from benefiting from other people's misfortunes. Do something for free for someone who needs it. Discount your fee—or cancel it altogether. Give some help without expecting payback. You'll be glad you did it.

- Perfect your union with the community by becoming involved in something just for fun—don't think about how it makes you look (nobody's looking), or whether it furthers your career (marketing has turned us all into silly little self-promoting publicity whores!) Just STOP already!

- Pursue the happiness of remembering things you have said you were going to do for others—and do them. Yeah, if you do X for me, then later I'll do Y for you— only we don't, we slickly move on and think it's been forgotten. Well it hasn't. What's been forgotten is why anybody ever trusted your word. Make good on your promises.

Other ideas of what to leave behind like drafty *Olde England*:

- Being aggrieved. You're the only one who remembers. Drop it.

- Needing to feel special. Really? What are you, four years old?! Make someone else feel special and bask in *their* happiness. It's even better!

- Vanity. You were never gorgeous and haven't improved. There, I've said it. Now say it to yourself so you can grow up. You'll love yourself for a whole new reason if you do.

- Xenophobia. Despite the current craze, your ancestors were no better than anybody else's. Sorry. Welcome to the kingdom of the unwashed masses. We've been waiting for you.

- Being a know-it-all. People have been letting you pretend to be smart for YEARS. Isn't it time you gave them a break from this game? Other people have ideas and understanding too. Really!

- And lastly, the deep-down, gnawing feeling of not being good enough. It's the root cause of everything I mentioned above (mostly) and it's unnecessary. You're as good as you need to be, and people far less fabulous than you have done marvelous things! Go ye, therefore, and do likewise.

Happy Independence Day!

ONE OF THE REASONS, *we are told by those who are supposed to know these things, that the Donald was able to weasel his way into our government was that a great teaming mass of the electorate is "aggrieved." They feel like they don't have as much as everyone else has, and they also think this situation is someone else's fault—namely illegal immigrants, educationally-advantaged "elites," and career politicians. All these skeevy folks have been taking what rightfully belongs to this great underclass of wronged individuals. Really? I disagree.*

While I am not "en masse" blaming every person who doesn't have what she thinks she deserves for her own situation, I do believe that before we go casting about for others to blame for our lot in life we should take a serious look at ourselves and make sure we have actually done all that we were capable of doing to achieve our goals.

IF YOU WANT IT

Why do we not have what we want? Is something working against us? Are we being cheated out of what is rightfully ours? I would answer with a definitive "Absolutely!" But not because any outside source robs us of anything—not at all. We rob ourselves.

Do you want a better life? There are steps to that end. A better job? Steps. More friends? Still more steps! Nothing on this earth just "happens." No one magically receives some benefice, some job, some love, great success, renown, peace of mind without following a well-crafted and hard-fought plan of action. But first, we have to WANT it. Now you say to me, "Of course I want it, I've been moaning about it for years!" Well, perhaps that's all you've been doing. . .

What we want, we pursue. What we desire, we work toward. Sometimes, what we simply moan about, what we feel deprived of, what we are most bitter because we lack—these are just convenient themes upon which to harp. It's so much easier to complain about not having something than it is to do the work required to achieve it. And if we can identify someone else who has what we want, or seems to—well then, that's even easier to grouse about. We don't have what we want because "they" are keeping it from us, because "they" are taking the good jobs, because "they" are secretly working against us, because. . . No. We DON'T WANT IT BADLY ENOUGH TO GO AND GET IT.

Some of the most effortless political conniving ever achieved was accomplished through identifying large groups of people (usually poor—either from societal causes they couldn't control or from their own lack of effort), who could be fooled into believing their own want or lack of accomplishment was due to some outside influence. Stalin demonized the Czar and convinced the Russian people to revolt, plunging the country into decades of misery and subjugation—far worse than anything foisted upon them by the Romanovs. Hitler fobbed off the financial woes of Germany onto the Jews, taking over the government and using his power to plunge the entire continent and nearly the world into ideological chaos and despair—and in the process, killed millions of those he deemed "less than." Joseph McCarthy used his Red scare to manipulate American's fears and to ruin the lives of thousands.

Today, we are upon the precipice of allowing ourselves to be used in a very similar way. Multitudes of otherwise fine upstanding citizens have been convinced, through years of clumsy scapegoating, finger-pointing, and just plain lies that they are somehow being "left out" of decision making in their government. They have been told that "experts," wonks," "elites," and otherwise well-meaning career civil servants are somehow working against the average citizen. That the people who've worked for years to learn the laws, master the protocols, bring together varied constituencies to form consensus, and generally make our government run are somehow "undeserving" of their place. No, these people are too privileged, too favored, too "elite," and the government ought to be run by "ordinary folks." Nothing could be farther from the truth.

A doctor is able to diagnose, a lawyer to make a contract, a legislator to make laws BECAUSE THEY WORKED FOR IT—earned the degrees, suffered the internships, and put in the time to achieve the mastery of their craft to be worthy of the job. No amount of my or your envy of the doctor's respect, the lawyer's income, or the legislator's influence is enough to de-legitimize their right to the position or to elevate us to their level in that particular trade, UNLESS WE DO THE WORK. If we want it like they wanted it, we can have it, but there are steps.

Likewise, a good many people have been convinced that the reason they have less than they feel is fair because of "illegal immigrants" or other outsiders. They've been told that their own religion is being affronted because people who don't share their beliefs are given rights and dignity. How much less popular would the bearers of these hateful insinuations be if they told the truth? That people have less than they want because they have abdicated their responsibility to vote effectively for people who will uphold their own rights—and that they have further failed to work hard enough to achieve their own goals in many instances. Failure to actually know the tenets of their own faith and its origins, and the workings of their own government make them even more susceptible to the lies of these peddlers of discontent and sowers of discord. A well-spoken, though poorly educated preacher can bring about a lot of real angst—demonizing people of different faiths and using ignorant fear for devious purposes. It happens every day. How many morality-preaching, fire-and-brimstone ministers have been found out to be secret perverts and criminals of all stripes? The same goes for our politicians. Just because a speaker throws the word "Constitution" around like holy water, does not mean they know what that document means—nor does it mean they are being honest with *you* about what it means, if that claimed content furthers their agenda.

No, we don't want what we think we want. For if we believe we can get what we want in some easy fashion (like persecution of fabricated enemies, or the election of hucksters with "easy" answers— "You're going to be winning so much, you're going to get tired of winning!"), well then, we'll take our comeuppances—we'll have what we deserve. But if we have to actually go through the steps, the study, the labor, the preparation, the self-education, the diligence, the cost, and the pain—then, THEN we don't really want it that bad.

There truly is *no free lunch*, and there is no substitute for hard work and *earning your place.*

SUFFERING THE DAILY INUNDATION *of indignities to our country and the constant feeling that the republic is sliding inevitably toward destruction takes a toll on your psyche. When the heat of summer adds its exclamation point to the mix, you sometimes just need to take stock of what still exists that is good and real.*

HIGH SUMMER

And the heat rises as it descends—it comes from every direction. The few gracious breezes that pass are teasing and coquettish—
Wondering if cool and calm will ever return, you laze, too drained to accomplish satisfying work.

The grass suffers, the clouds are indistinct, animals mope drearily in the distance. "Hotter at eventide than e'er was noon," the pattern is confused. And the countryside longs for a thunderstorm, but none is coming. Bees swim through the atmosphere, as if transformed into fish by the thickness of the humidity.

When bathed in the sun, we dreamed of Fall and long for winter's chill. When gripped with cold and the icy wind's whine, we pine for Springtime, and the solid warmth of summer. Never content in the moment, we beg the question of the existence of heaven. For what temperature or clime could satisfy us for eternity? That endless succession of days could never suffice our fickle nature. Would not a continuous string of warm or cold days be, instead, hell? What relief would we crave? What could we complain about if we were told we had achieved paradise?

It is for this reason we must seek our heaven here—cling to the pleasant aspects of existence and shun to mention the nagging discomforts. For it is by this selective recognition that we craft one destination or the other—either the tedious and miserable plain where all is itch and chafe, or the delectable grove where soft living is offered and accepted. But how, you may ask, does one construct this unclouded day? Purposefully, dear one. Carefully, my sweet.

Choose to savor the garden's offerings, get your hands dirty in the soil, walk in the woods and smell the musty wonder. Notice the vibrant colors, sniff the flowers, drink coolly with friends, lounge and nap in the shade, pet a small animal, visit a new and beautiful locale. Swim if you can! Run if you dare! Drive with the windows down, sleep on a screened porch for a change, stay up and take in the summer sky. Learn something new, make a friend, put down that damn phone for a few hours!

As you begin to highlight in your perception the pure and right, as you mindfully discard possibilities to complain, as you smile, as you laugh, as you sigh or even cry a little, you cannot help but see a kinder landscape as your home, you'll have no choice but to be happy—even just a little at a time. It is inescapable.

And when the inevitable scowl drops by to whine of the heat and humidity, to pass on harsh tidings, to criticize and needle, to surreptitiously ladle you into a foul mood — listen patiently but refuse to add to the plaint— you have chosen your reward, and they theirs.

SOMEONE HAS TO PAY. *Disloyalty to the American principles of decency and equality, dishonesty to the point of utter treachery, greed, corruption, the foment of hatred and bigotry, the elevation of sheer ignorance as a virtue and the denigration of real experts who have worked to make a difference in the world—all this deserves a day of reckoning, and it IS coming.*

THE LURE OF NOVELTY

Don't just stand there, Do something! Like what? Anything, just DO something! Well, that might just be the problem. . . You see, we are obsessed with busyness, obsessed with novelty, obsessed with staying occupied with something—when we might be better off sitting idly and thinking. At least we wouldn't be making the situation worse.

The celebrity mill would have us believe there's no such thing as bad publicity, that the only thing worse than being talked about is NOT being talked about, that causing a meaningless distraction is as worthwhile as actually accomplishing something. Well, in serious matters, as well as in those issues relating to our souls, that is decidedly NOT the case. Substance matters. Intent matters. Strategy matters. Character matters. Intelligence matters. Diplomacy, steadfastness, integrity, skill, and class ALL MATTER.

How often have we seen a celebrity scandal arise only to hear later that it was completely fabricated just to keep that public personality in the glow of the spotlight? How often do we notice a political operative make a statement just to elicit a response from the opposing side? How often nowadays does the very president of the United States (such as he is) make a nonsensical proclamation that can be for no other reason than to draw attention away from other, even less flattering scandals? (I'll go on and say it, the Russia investigation). But, in the long run, just how effective is this tactic? Have the people who matter really forgotten about Russia? Have the people who refuse to see ANY of this president's flaws ever even taken notice of Russia Gate? And if both of these are true, what possible good can drawing attention to another ugly blemish on the reputation of this administration do? Well, if you've made the ultimate existential blunder of believing your own press, you might believe the cumulative damage to your image doesn't really matter because you're bulletproof— indestructible, so pure in motive and action that the opinion of mere mortals cannot harm you. It's the ultimate game of "sticks and stones." I'm sorry, but in the real world—and ultimately that's where we all eventually realize we've been living—cumulative damage, image destruction, motive demonization, and the uncovering of the reality of soullessness DOES matter.

A TRUMP DIARY

Nicolai Ceausescu lived in a fantasy world where the slings and arrows of fortune could not touch him—until they did. Al Capone was invincible—until he wasn't. Boss Tweed, Roy Cohn, Joe McCarthy, George Wallace, and Richard Nixon— all enjoyed the illusion that they were somehow "untouchable," that the forces which opposed them were so incompetent, corrupt, clueless, or powerless that they couldn't be beaten. But they were beaten. And, in the end, it is this lesson we must remember and heed. The scofflaws and cheaters of the world are given their time to despoil and plunder, and then comes judgement day.

We are called to bring about the comeuppance of those who have no conscience and claim no personal moral code. We must remind the untouchables that their day of reckoning is fast approaching— and when that day has come at last, we need to do more than punish, we are called to remind. We must remind the world what integrity is. We must remind the world what compassion is, what honor is, what kindness, selflessness, mercy, goodwill, uprightness, and well-meaning generosity really is.

There is no honor in acting simply to cover our tracks. There is no justification for stirring up hatred and civil strife just to confound the resolve of our political opponents. There is no way to rationalize acting in bad faith just because you think the opposing side is misguided—winning is not its own reward, you need to be right. And the way you show you are right is by helping more people with your ideas than the alternative side could ever do.

S. TIMOTHY GLASSCOCK

Don't just stand there! Do something— but the RIGHT something. And if you can't do the right thing, sit down and shut up and pray somebody else WILL do it!

The end of this giant fiasco is fast approaching, but we the loyal opposition must be ready and prepared to make things right, not just different.

HAPPINESS MATTERS—*it matters a lot. And keeping up your strength to fight the good fight is not enough if you are allowing yourself to embrace a defeatist attitude. Happiness is not a continual feeling of elation, or even a state of being that you strive for and, after much struggle, achieve, never to be unhappy again. Instead it is a constant, renewing decision to see the good that remains and use that reality to keep yourself in a state of positivity. Happiness persists through hardship, because it is an essential trait of victory. When Winston Churchill made his "V for victory" sign, most of the time, he was smiling!*

CHOOSING HAPPINESS

I am constantly amazed at people and their individual reactions to circumstances. You have privileged, relatively wealthy, healthy, employed, loved, and empowered individuals who struggle to find the will to face each day—I place myself in this camp. Then, not infrequently, I see underprivileged, mistreated, poor, unemployed or underemployed, lonely struggling heroes who face it all with grace and determination.

How? What? Is there an explanation? Yes, I believe there is. Choice. Happiness is not a function of wealth— the world is full of miserable people with money. Happiness is not dictated by health— read "Tuesdays with Morrie" and witness a dying man passing on hope by living his final days with grace and optimism. Does privilege guarantee it? Watch the meltdowns on continuous loop in the world of rock icons, billionaires' children, and aging child stars. Must one have the love of their lives to be content? Nope. Single, widowed, conventual, elderly, living in seclusion— there are examples of all of these situations displaying some of the most well-adjusted individuals on earth.

Just like kindness, just like industry—like charity, patience, prudence, empathy, understanding, forgiveness, and determination—happiness is a choice. You can let your finances decide. You can decide you're not allowed to be happy until you find your "soulmate," until you retire, until you finish raising your kids, until your get a divorce, until you're successful enough to be a household name. All of these are copouts and roadblocks to your destiny.

Choose to be happy NOW. I'm not even going to remind you of your personal blessings BECAUSE THEY ARE NOT NECESSARY TO THIS ADMONITION. Don't look for happiness, don't pray for happiness, don't long for it, don't work for it, don't ask, don't bargain, don't bother. Choose it and make it a reality. It is in your power. You had it all along. Now take it and don't allow anyone or anything take it from you. I'm right there with you, choosing to BE happy.

PERHAPS THE HARDEST REALITY *of the Trump fiasco has been that WE did this. Not specifically those of us who voted for the Democratic nominee, but those who chose to make a "protest vote" (unbelievably irresponsible in retrospect), or those who (and I cannot get over how many of these I actually know) voted . . .for . . .Trump. There were hundreds of instances in the past where you found yourself at odds with a friend's political leanings, but you never found it such an egregious lapse of judgment that you thought of re-considering the friendship. But now—with this particular decision having been proved as such a colossal mistake—you find yourself thinking "How could so-and-so do such a thing?!" I needed to think about that.*

MANAGING EXPECTATIONS

Did you ever have a friend who disappointed you? Family member? Co-worker? It's something we all face sooner or later but keeping a reasonable handle on our expectations of others is important.

We are all limited by unseen modifiers—some of which others know about or can intuit are there, but they can never know the extent and the strength of these modifiers. What do I mean by modifiers? Things that limit a person's ability to be effective or to see the world clearly— things inherent in their psyche that only they feel the brunt of.

Fear, dysfunction, addiction, mental illness— all these things and more are invisible limiters to some of your friends', family members', and coworkers', functioning. I'm not saying these issues are fine to be left alone and are natural. I believe strongly in our need to overcome such obstacles, but only the actual sufferer can affect this change, and only if they know they are affected. If it's an issue they either aren't aware of, or just aren't sharing with you, there's nearly nothing you can do to help. One thing you might be doing that's a big hindrance, however, is holding them to expectations they cannot meet because of limitations you cannot see. This is a sure-fire way to increase someone's suffering while really just feeling sorry for yourself.

I have been guilty of holding people to standards set for myself— having truly not considered that others might not be capable of functioning exactly in the way I am capable.

Why didn't so-and-so see that I was hurting and needed comfort? Why couldn't X see that he hurt my feelings? Why couldn't Y avoid seeming insensitive to Z? Why can't A just move on with her life?

First, we must accept that no one owes us anything. No one is required to react in a way we find appropriate. People react to and interact with the world based upon their own perception, and that perception was formed over many years in circumstances you can only guess at.

Was X shown love or empathy while growing up? If not, he'll find it much harder, if not impossible to show it to others. Has Y been hurt repeatedly by those she thought were friends? If so, she'll find it difficult to open herself to new friends—maybe for the rest of her life.

People who were never made to feel worthy may spend years attempting to prove that they are special, or talented, or smart. With a need this urgent driving them, they'll likely not notice that they can never seem to spare a compliment or kind word for you— it simply will not naturally occur to them. Even people we think we know intimately may harbor burdens that keep them from having what we consider healthy reactions to the world around them. But again, our personal opinions regarding healthy response are not necessarily binding upon others.

It helps to remove the focus from what others are doing and focus on our own actions, our own motives, our own shortcomings in dealing with others. Firstly, it's the only thing we can truly see clearly—because we are most likely to know our own issues and hindrances. Secondly, because our own actions are the only things we are able to and allowed to change. If we can be sure that we ourselves are acting in love, generosity, and kindness, then the reactions of others will be more likely to mirror those intentions.

S. TIMOTHY GLASSCOCK

"I'm starting with the man in the mirror. I'm asking him to change his ways, and no message could've been any clearer—if you want to make the world a better place, take a look at yourself and then make the change."

— Michael Jackson, "Man in the Mirror."

(While recent revelations may cast doubt on the singer's adherence to this sentiment, the sentiment stands.)

ONE OF THE PRIMARY JUSTIFICATIONS *offered for why Trump is fit to be president is that he has been so "successful" in business. Yes, that's exactly what we keep hearing. Successful. Is it considered success if you end up with a large sum of money, but you leave a path of destruction and misery in your wake? Is it possible to consider yourself a success if you start out with a larger advantage financially than nearly anyone you can name yet still don't end up actually any richer than a number of people who started with nothing? We have migrated to an unsustainable definition of what "success" means. And while I am a great skeptic of both the "fact" that Donald Trump should be considered a "success," as well as the assertion that a "successful businessman" is necessarily qualified to lead the world's largest economy, I also think that before we judge the Donald, we should take a look at ourselves and make sure we are holding both him, and ourselves, to the same standards.*

EVALUATING SUCCESS

Are you successful? What does it mean?

I tend to think that there is such a thing as long-term success, which we have to think about in more abstract terms, and short-term success, which can mean many things on many different days. Success today may mean finishing a project by the deadline, while success yesterday was simply making it through the day without careening into despair.

We know now that certain measures of success are faulty— measuring our personal progress against other people, expecting to get the same amount of work done *every* time we start, creating an equally impressive creative product with this particular group of collaborators as that which we experienced with the last team. These are completely irrational expectations. Other people have different skills, training, advantages and disadvantages, support systems, goals, and motivations—meaning comparisons are impossible since the variables can never be equal. Different days bring changes in mood, weather, other people's willingness or ability to contribute, and just plain old chance! A different group of people brings a multitude of varying factors that cannot be quantified—so every new project is a whole new world.

So how do we judge our approach to progress?

Here are a few possibilities:

- Was my whole focus on the work? Without this assertion in the affirmative, you simply cannot know what is possible.

- Did I approach the work without prejudice? Sometimes we doom ourselves to failure at the outset of our work with a bad attitude, "This thing is not a good idea. Why did I agree to this? These people don't care! I am just not up to this." Remove these stumbling blocks or you are destined to end up on the rocks.

- Did I use all the tools I've been given? "I know I could ask Bob for help with this, but I don't feel like having to share decision making."

- Have I prepared myself to succeed? Did you do the necessary prep work? Study? Planning? Brainstorming? If not, maybe today is a prep day and tomorrow is the real start.

- Do I want to succeed? What do you mean, do I want to succeed? Well, I'll tell you— I have witnessed people who continually defeated themselves with failing at all the above prerequisites time and again. These people were not stupid, they had every skill that people around them who were accomplishing great work possessed. They showed up seemingly ready to go, yet never rose off the runway. After examining their failure over and over, I could conclude nothing other than that these folks DID NOT WANT TO SUCCEED. I really think it is a big problem.

With success comes notice. With notice comes scrutiny. With scrutiny comes pressure, and stress. There is very little strain involved in plodding along in mediocrity—people tend to look away, to leave you to your failure and focus on people who make them glad to be watching. It's embarrassing to stare too long at someone flailing and making no progress, and it takes a really exceptional individual to stop and say, "You seem to be having some difficulties with this, let me help you," because this also involves a risk of rejection, anger, and conflict. It's easier to mind your own business and *let them fail.*

Daily, I coach myself to want to succeed, to prepare to achieve great things, to use every advantage I can find, to approach my task with expectations of greatness, and to focus on nothing but a positive outcome. My standard is my own personal best, and I measure only against that ruler.

I hope this helps somebody! It helps me.

THIS PRESIDENT HAS NO MANNERS. *He cares nothing for protocols. He thinks that by breaking traditions and by dashing expectations of decency and decorum he is somehow "shaking up" the old ways. Well, the "old ways" have been developed, in many instances, in order to create a framework around which people can organize their thoughts and actions. This way, different parties can hopefully interact in a civil and dignified way that assists governments, internal agencies, and societies with wildly different traditions in getting along with one another. To cast these protocols and processes aside merely because you cannot be bothered to learn them is to prove that you are not suited for the job of president. This is a primary feature of the long-time cliché of the "ugly American" who used to travel to foreign countries having not done enough research to find out how to get along in these places and simply expecting others to accommodate what you are used to. Well, the "ugly American" is in charge now, and the world is not amused.*

S. TIMOTHY GLASSCOCK

ACTING IN LOVE

Manners are very important. When I was young, I listened to a lot of admonitions regarding my manners: "If you can't say anything nice, don't say anything at all," "Never say anything you wouldn't repeat in front of your grandmother," "Do unto others as you would have them do unto you." "Think before you speak, and think twice before you act," "Look at the situation from the other person's perspective," and lastly, the hardest one to follow, but probably the truest yardstick, "In all that you do, be sure you are acting in love."

Now I understand the difficulty inherent in these little adages—they are only strictly correct in polite and well-meaning society. When you are dealing with rogues and cads, they'll get you eaten alive-if you follow them truly, you'll never say anything negative at all and there are truly times when the only right thing to do is to speak to contradict those in the wrong. So, it's true that not all words "spoken in love" are pleasantries. However, there are a judgmental few whose beliefs urge them to speak chastisingly to others in criticism of their very personage. The phrase "Hate the sin, but love the sinner," comes to mind. This juicy little license to discriminate has cropped up on the lips of a good many otherwise intelligent people and it truly makes absolutely zero sense.

First of all, people have a variety of personal beliefs—creeds, traditions, ethnic traits, and sets of religious tenets—and they can neither be predicted nor expected to josh with our own. So, having said that, how can we distinguish between what can rightfully be said as a criticism in love and what kind of comment makes us downright bigoted. Well, I think I have an answer.

Any comment criticizing the very being or nature of another person—demonizing their essence as opposed to their actions—is wrong. Generalizations about ethnicity, gender, or sexual orientation are, for this reason, out of bounds. They are akin to condemning a man for having brown hair and everyone understands why that is ridiculous and wrong-headed.

What non-fawning comments, then, are acceptable in mannered society. I believe comments that critique actions and words are wholly appropriate. When anyone causes dishonor, emotional pain, or personal harm to others, they should be rebuked—and I would aver that this rebuke could indeed be given in as kind a manner as possible, i.e. given in love. The *ad hominem* attacks on individuals described in the previous paragraph are abhorrent and should be called out, and contrary to my dearly departed grandmother's admonitions, I might even support omitting the love in that rebuke.

That's just me. What about you?

FAKE NEWS. *We hear it every day. Any news that doesn't comport with the image Trump has in his head of what he is and what he is doing is labeled "fake." Then, there is the fake news his regime creates. Whether you're watching Kelly Anne Conway answer everything except the question she's been asked, or Sean Spicer try to bully the press into acquiescence, or listening to Sarah Huckabee Sanders dole out one non-sequitur after another, you can easily get the gist of the fact that "truth" doesn't mean a lot to this president. Bill Clinton was roundly ridiculed for commenting that it depended on what the definition of "is" is. Well, that little bon mot is a toddler's dream of a fib compared to the Olympic sport of lying we are now witnessing from Big Orange and his henchmen. Never fear. There IS such a thing as truth. It has not ceased to exist simply because they refuse to employ it or to use it as any measuring stick for the veracity of what they have to say.*

WHAT IS REAL

I live I Kentucky, so the first Saturday in May is Derby Day and our city is everything horses and Bourbon. Lots of people relish this ritual and can't wait to dive into the glitz and hullabaloo. Not me. As an introvert, I truly dread large crowds and having to be "seen." I can't think of anything more dreadful than hours upon end of being surrounded by strangers in fancy dress, fueled by gambling and alcohol. But if your daily life is fairly dull, and most of ours are, you have to understand the desire to break up the monotony and cut loose now and again. It's just natural.

We seek novelty, we crave variety, we are creatures of the smorgasbord—and there's nothing wrong with that tendency. But we have to differentiate between the appetizer and the main course—we have to know that, while the dessert is tantalizing, the main course is where the nutritional value lies. We are not made up of the splash of fancy, the decadent splurge, the one-time spree—we are composed of the everyday and rightly so. While our day to day is often seemingly mundane, it is the solid and true core of our being. Those people you struggle with to create a project — your fellow teachers, office staff, or dock workers—they are what creates your true substance and are more important than can be estimated,

Your intimate circle, your trusted compadres—these are the building blocks of true life! While we need the distraction of vacation, parties, and junkets, what is the true US at our core is the everyday and reliable. The people and places you know inside and out, the values of support and empathy you've developed through interaction with these touchstones of your existence are what is real.

Dream of a trip to paradise. Go to a wild social event. Throw a party. Take a vacation. But remember that home, family, friends, and something to contribute are what make us who we are. These are what is real.

I am holed up in my cabin for a day or two, and what keeps returning to me are my thoughts of how lucky I am to have my wild, busy life and the crowd of weirdos that keep me spinning all day every day. I am thankful for my solid, predictable, somewhat mundane, but truly quality life. I am glad that I know what and who are real, and I am happy with that fact.

Gratitude today.

WE'VE HAD BAD PRESIDENTS. *Some, like Ronald Reagan, were at least cunning enough to create a false sense of comfort while they padded the pocketbooks of the wealthy and leveraged our future in order to pump up that "bidness climate." Others, like George W. Bush, were seemingly innocuous in their presentation—a good-natured buffoon, not really in charge of anything, but buoyed along by the gargoyles surrounding him and the steady stream of "rah-rah, Murica!" that his followers found so soothing. Clandestine cooperation with dictators, arms deals in the dark with sketchy intent—all these skated by whilst co-conspirators hummed "America the Beautiful" in the background. But this . . . THIS . . .is different. Where we are now is a hopeless landscape, covered in ominous, sticky, alien goo that portends a truly devastating climax. This is the "upside down," through the looking glass, Bizzaro America, where the party that used to be obsessed with fighting the "Ruskies" is now completely comfortable with their de facto party head living in Vladimir Putin's back pocket. You can almost hear the raspy, guttural voice of the disaster movie announcer saying "In a WORLD, where the party of law-and-order no longer cares what is legal, where the party of 'the shining city on a hill' is content with a steaming shit-hole in the valley, where*

nothing the Dear Leader does can be wrong . . . "It's quite easy to despair. And when you do, you run for the comforting embrace of poetry and scripture. Only what you find that fits the situation. . . is rarely comforting.

THE CENTER CANNOT HOLD

Round and round she goes . . .
We pray for a stop, but none is forthcoming.
In our brave new country,
The baby seals club themselves to death.
The down and out elect the downright ridiculous.
Only he who spun the roulette can say where we land,
and he was wearing a blindfold of ignorance.

We find ourselves bouncing from pole to pole,
shiny objects inside the pinball machine.
The lever is pulled and off we go again!
But what is the endgame?
How do we win? How does anyone?
He who dies with the most toys.
There are 300-odd million toys in this amusement,
and none are sacred or of any value to the players in the
game.

The scoreboards have all changed places;
The numbers make no sense.
Promises kept are slow comfort, whatever benefit to come is
marching behind an army of woe.
The weakest are played like pawns of paper and the strong
are arguing over the rules of the game.

Down is up, left is right, and rules only temporary anyway—till someone needs new ones. And new pawns, and rooks, and knights.
The queen is alone and the king is grazing in the field like Nebuchadnezzar.

"And they shall drive thee from men, and thy dwelling shall be with the beasts of the field: they shall make thee to eat grass as oxen, and seven years shall pass over thee, until thou knowest that the most High ruleth in the kingdom of men, and giveth it to whomsoever he will." — (KJV) Daniel 4:32

THERE'S A REALLY FUNNY GEICO COMMERCIAL *where a guy has fallen into quicksand and a grumpy, disinterested cat sits idly by while he cries for help and sinks to his doom. The voiceover says "If you're a cat, you IGNORE people. It's what you do!" The announcer goes on to explain that what GEICO does is save people money on insurance. It's good advertising. But it also mimics the attitude of a great number of citizens who simply cannot be bothered to keep up with politics, or voting, or even recognizing that these things matter. It's really maddening, especially since the more people there are with this "nothing you can do will change things" attitude, the more it becomes TRUE.*

TAKING A STAND

"I'm not political." "It won't do any good." "It's too late now." "Nobody's listening." "I don't want to upset anyone." "I have a lot of friends who disagree." "You shouldn't talk politics or religion."

You've heard them all, and they are ALL copouts! It has been said, "If you don't stand for something, you'll fall for anything." This is true for many reasons.

"I'm not political." Really? You don't try to convince anyone to change what they are doing or saying? Ever? You don't weigh in on where the office should go for lunch? No opinion on what the church service project should be? You don't know who is going to be given a task and do nothing, so you try to keep that person from being in charge. You don't try to get lackadaisical parents to control their children when their behavior affects your own kids? Right. You, my friend, are full of it. We are all political—it is human nature and this excuse is a simple attempt to evade responsibility for stepping up and taking a position.

It won't do any good." Au contraire! The simplest moves and sometimes just speaking out DOES indeed make a difference every day. Ask Erin Brockovich. Ask the University priest in Czech Republic who brought down the communist government. Ask Martin Luther King, Jr. and all his acolytes. Ask Rosa Parks. Ask Harriet Tubman. YOU make a difference. If you refuse to act, you are complicit in the tragic outcome.

Nobody's listening." People ARE listening — people do change their minds, it just takes the right amount of evidence and repetition. Jesus told a parable about the judge who was besieged by a widow demanding he deliver her justice in her suit—and while this judge was corrupt and "feared neither God nor man," he DID intercede in her case and gave her satisfaction JUST BECAUSE SHE REFUSED TO

BE SILENT! This is not an unrealistic story—the squeaky wheel DOES get the grease.

I don't want to upset anyone." Really? They don't mind walking all over you! Someone is not afraid to upset your faction in society—and you're content to let them get by with it and sit in silence. I do not believe anyone is ruled by that instinct. This is an excuse for LAZINESS. Your inaction has upset as many people as your action. Forget about what other people think and let them decide what they are going to do. YOU DECIDE FOR YOU!

I have a lot of friends who disagree." And they will still be your friends when you are done expressing yourself— if they aren't, they WERE NEVER YOUR FRIENDS. There were friends with differences of opinion in the civil war, but it had to be fought. There were differences of opinion about the women's suffrage movement—should they have remained silent to be polite to their "disapproving" friends? This is an excuse to keep from opening up uncomfortable discussions. This is a part of life, GET OVER IT.

You shouldn't talk politics or religion." No. You shouldn't force your opinion upon anyone regarding politics or religion. But speaking out IS YOUR RIGHT AND YOUR DUTY. Get out there! Open your mouth. Change the world! Or. . . Forfeit your right to complain . . . forever. Really.

GOTTA HAVE A TIME-OUT! *Gotta take some time to reaffirm my personal beliefs and stop listening the call of the wild Bullshit Bird. The "values" being touted by Big Orange and his minions are not values at all—they're tired slogans, trite memorized bible verses, "I know you are, but what am I?" The only way to keep from falling into true black despair is to return to the 'self' for a while and re-dedicate yourself to real values, real patriotism, real humanity.*

WHAT SUCCESS IS

A dear old friend of mine has had a refrigerator magnet as long as I can remember that says "Happiness is not having what you want but wanting what you have." I've noticed that my initial bemused reaction to the quote as a 21-year-old has grown into an acceptance of it as a real truth. In fact, it's one of my unofficial personal mottos.

We start out with goals influenced by an amazing array of unreliable sources that volley us from side to side and obscure important guideposts that could steady our path. Advice from Mom and Dad, elevated (or decreased) expectations of teachers, perceptions of friends, advertising campaigns, movies and tv, and just plain old misunderstandings from the dark recesses of our childhood all conspire to create a misty maze from which even the most well-adjusted young person can scarce escape with any clear idea of a way forward.

Parents' understandable desire for their children to "succeed" often leads to pressuring a young person into a seemingly lucrative field, regardless of their aptitude or personal desire for that career. Teachers, myself included, often see their own career as having been a magical unfolding of fate that placed them into the "perfect" job to follow their inclinations and to have a positive effect on coming generations. The competing perceptions of your peer group include everything from parent worship to the desire for social advancement to fantasies of escaping what has been your climate-controlled cocoon for 18 years. Stereotypes in media show smiling happy doctors with knowing cameo soliloquies, dedicated yet near impoverished school teachers, downtrodden factory workers, struggling farmers losing their family homestead, and twenty-somethings with nebulous part-time jobs living in sprawling New York apartments and spending most of their days lounging in trendy coffee shops with their equally inexplicably carefree friends.

We walk out of that fog as teens and into a job market where skeleton-crew-run businesses expect heroic performance from their handful of slightly paid employees with little training and zero support or understanding. Promotion is based on everything *except* what we were told. Often, people who do the job flawlessly are prevented from advancing because the continuous influx of new workers is incapable of the simplest tasks. Those less successful are allowed to apply for and achieve higher positions, both to get them out of the department, and to allow the undertrained management to avoid uncomfortable firings.

Grade inflation, job availability overestimation by colleges, poor academic advising, formulaic career counseling, and just plain deceit come together in a maelstrom of uncertainty that make choosing the wrong career path the most likely outcome.

Finding a life partner is no less fraught with obstacles. Buying a house? Finding a reliable vehicle (if you need one), managing student loans, credit cards, surprise expenses, navigating banking and loan approval—make life far more complicated than anyone could ever have explained to you. This is completely without beginning to discuss having children (which is more treacherous by half than everything we've mentioned.)

So how do you find your way?

What makes you happy? What do you do well?
Who is your friend without wavering?
What do you really NEED?
How little can you get by with? Would you be happier with fewer material things in a different location?
Are you taking time to think things through? Have you analyzed it on paper?

What's making you UNhappy? Who could you do WITHOUT?

Are you feeding your spirit? What are you doing that helps SOMEONE ELSE?

Are you doing anything that fulfills you in any way? COULD you be?

After you answer a few of these things, and practice following your heart, along with solid planning and analysis of your options, you might find a way toward a more reasonable facsimile of happiness. How long does it take? So far, 50 years.

Meditation, time with friends, a hobby or two, constant reinforcement of personal goals and their importance, and striving to do good as well as to do well—these are all helping me have a meaningful journey. And remember, it IS a journey.

WE MAKE OURSELVES SICK. *It's true! Doctors in several well-researched studies have determined that our mental state—what we focus on, positive or negative—can MAKE US SICK. Well, if any situation is twisted enough to actually produce physical sickness in a population, it would be the election of Trump.*

NOT FEELING WELL

You know those little nagging sicknesses that you get, but you can't ever seem to completely get over? You have a few good days, and then BLAM you feel just as bad as when it first hit you. I've had water behind my eardrums for weeks and no matter what I do, I can't recover. Some days it seems to be leaving, but then comes right back like it never improved at all. I took a spate of antibiotics after it was discovered that one ear was infected, but here I am

Our country is in the same boat. Our sickness? Racism. Jealousy. Selfishness. Sometimes we think we have just a touch of it, but really, it's a chronic thing and we never get over it. We first realized our sickness in the 18th century when abolitionists began talking about the evil of slavery. They diagnosed our problem really accurately when they noted that the presence of slavery was destroying the moral compass of our populace.

This conscience treatment resulted in a lot of fighting among the framers of the constitution who thought a really good purgative was in order. Instead, we ignored the disease and hoped it would go away on its own. Then, in the early 1800s, there was much ado about "slave states" and "free states," where we basically argued that the body politic wasn't truly sick unto death as long as we had a few good members. "One good strong arm still works, so the patient must be on the mend."

Well, that was basically our first serious bout of diagnostic malfeasance and it led, inevitably, to the Civil War, which the sickest members of the body called the "War of Northern Aggression." Needless to say, that war dragged on and on until one particularly prescient doctor made an emancipation proclamation, finally treating the most painful symptom of our collective malady. The war ended and the reformers won, but the disease fought back, killed the president, and since our country failed to do the physical therapy that was "reconstruction," the disease and its symptoms lived on, despite the drastic measures taken to eradicate it.

We coddled our sickness in various parts of the body with "Jim Crow" laws, assuring ourselves that the doctor didn't know what he was doing, and we were fine. Before we could realize that we were still violently ill, we had to lose another president, and that painful loss empowered the remaining leader to act. So, in the early 20th century, some other well-meaning medical practitioners came up with the "Civil Rights Act" of 1964, and this empowered president got it passed.

Years of "treatments" (killings, trials, legislation, public debate, protest, and political activity) later, we thought the election of a black president might be the signal that we were finally cured. The uprising of hatred, innuendo, vicious hyperbole, and opposition from people who claimed racism had nothing to do with this inflammation finally showed us that we were horribly wrong to think the treatments had been even remotely effective. There were healthy members of the body, where the majority of people tried to act without prejudice and malice. But there were also still pockets of infection where subtle racism (and its accompanying irritation, xenophobia) were rampant, and our failure to recognize them had allowed them to fester.

Then, along came a candidate for the highest office in the land who spoke in a manner which appealed to the sickest instincts in us. The righteous "US" versus the insidious and untrustworthy "THEM," the indictment of the doctors as poisoners, the discriminated-against as discriminators, the majority as slighted minority—these simplistic and seemingly easily seen-through rhetorical flourishes were somehow embraced as a "new message." But there is nothing new about this message.

It is as old as **suspicion** in the garden of Eden. "God is lying to you—he says if you eat that fruit you'll die, but really, it will make you just like him!" "*The media say they're reporting the facts, but it's just fake news!*"

It is as old as **jealousy** in the prodigal son "I have been faithful in everything, but to this faithless son you give a ring and kill the fatted calf!?" "**The hard-working middle class are getting the shaft, while public assistance rewards lazy people!**"

As old as **intimidation of the weak.** "Bow down to me, Daniel, or I will cast you into the lion's den!" "*Chuck, if the media keep referring to our press secretary in that way, we're going to have to rethink our relationship.*" Or "**No, I'm not going to take a question from you, you're fake news!**"

As old as **lack of charity** passing on the opposite side of the road to avoid touching a wounded and dying man, while claiming you're trying to preserve ritual purity. *Or banning people of a different religion but calling it something else.*

As old as **corruption,** taking 30 pieces of silver to betray an unpopular figure. *Or confirming a nominee to a post because she donated millions to your campaign.*

Nope, there's nothing new here. Our sickness is alive and well, and we'll do ANYTHING to keep from getting better.

THE PRESIDENT IS A RACIST. *I don't have to have him on the record admitting it (after all, we can't even get him on the record admitting that he's not 6'3" and 239 lbs.!), the evidence is irrefutable. Tone deaf proclamations that there was "violence on many sides" of a de facto KLAN RALLY, comments demeaning black politicians in ways no one else would have dared, not to mention the decades-old allegations he sought ways not to rent to African Americans – all these instances, and many more, come together to paint a portrait of a person with attitudes about race most people thought had been relegated to the ash heap of history. We can't be soft on hatred. We can't hedge our bets on fighting fascism. There are those who are on the cutting edge of this fight, and I'm right behind them.*

WHAT LOVE DEMANDS

The first tenant of the Hippocratic Oath is "do no harm, the "Golden Rule" of Jesus is "do unto others," Hillary Clinton quotes an old Methodist stand by, "Do all the good you can, by all the means you can, for as long as you can." And all of these standards are noble in their own way. But we find ourselves faced today with enemies whose malice is unmistakable as well as unquenchable.

The white supremacists who have dared to raise their shameless heads into the light today are "not your Father's KKK." They are using the tools of modernity such as the internet and social media, they are hob-knobbing with key players in government (thanks to the election of our new grand wizard, *er* president), they are crafting a nuanced message based on marketing research and civil infiltration techniques—these people want to be a part of our society into perpetuity. But in order to confront and defeat them, we must remember one thing: a rose (or perhaps in this instance, a turd) by any other name smells the same.

Recently, we have seen the insidious tendency to equate hate groups with the organizations that fight them, to make such comments as "shared blame" and "violence on *many sides.*" Well, these attempts are just what you thought they were—obfuscation and smoke screens. Designed to provide cover for the evil of racism and intolerance. We can't be fooled by such amateurish attempts at false equivalency, because there are huge swaths of the population who are just dim enough to swallow this silly farce whole. These laughable excuses must be shamed and booed off the public stage.

"Antifa" is a group that counters racism in all its forms. They show up at gatherings of white supremacist organizations and racist protests all over the country to protect regular citizens from the tactics of bigotry. Antifa also tracks racist leaders and their activities, keeping the larger public informed about what these seedy, bottom-feeding, menaces to society are planning and how to show up in force to counter their mischief. There have been times when Antifa has been drawn into violent confrontations with these racist groups, creating the tendency to equate them with their nemeses— this false equivalency is a mistake. Antifa and all other counter-bigotry groups must be supported. Always supported. If they make mistakes in judgement, then individual perpetrators can be prosecuted (just like members of any group), but the organizations themselves are CRUCIAL to the survival of our country — especially during an unprecedented period where our own president cannot be counted upon to disavow the evil of racism and seems not to know the difference between racists and anti-racists.

How can we support people who may resort to violence? Because we support the actions of the Allies in WW II, because we supported the Union Army during the American Civil War, because we support the police when they confront mob violence or bank robbers. Because Barry Goldwater was not wrong when he stated, "Extremism in the cause of liberty is no vice!" While the principles he was defending with this statement have been proven anathema to modern society, the statement on its own was never more prescient. Sometimes you can't just make a statement. Sometimes you have to fight.

Love demands our full measure of devotion. Love demands commitment and loyalty—sometimes even commitment to actions we'd normally disavow. While civil discourse is the goal, violent confrontation is often a tool of the unjust, and they must know that there are people who will bring the fight right back to them if they use that tool. If we are only willing to offer our words in defense of our fellow man, it is possible that our love for them consists only of words as well. We must do what love demands and go the full distance.

Defend the weak and vulnerable, speak out against hatred and bigotry, shame those who seek to harm others, and work for justice in all possible ways. But also, be ready to defend those whose actions are bolder than ours in defense of the same great ideals— they are fitted for situations where we ourselves might have been found inadequate. When the time comes, love recognizes that often the only discernible difference between warring factions is what they are fighting for— and make no mistake, that is what matters. Anti-fascists, we've got your back.

WE GET THE GOVERNMENT WE DESERVE.

Really?! I think we get the government we THINK we deserve. We, collectively, have a self-esteem problem. Years of being fat-shamed by size '0's in magazines, fawning feature stories about self-made teenage millionaires, re-touched photos in high school yearbooks that make Cosmopolitan look like a parent-teacher club newsletter—all this breeds a sense of being less-than. It's just not true.

YOU ARE ENOUGH

You look out at the room...faces blank and uncomprehending. You make your case, lay out your argument, explain the lesson of the day—nothing, vague boredom. You try to cook a nice meal, it tastes like something from a third-rate cafeteria. You are late for a meeting, you miss a deadline, you make a comment that draws winces or smirks.

All of these situations happen to us all— or something equivalent—it's the human condition. Next time, the classroom will seem to move as a well-oiled unit, the students smiling and open faced, the responses engaging and connected. The meal will turn out like you planned it, the meeting will show your brilliance, your work will be praised, your contributions will once again impress. How do I know this? The wheel turns, the seasons come and go, the phases of the moon affect as they will, and we can but react to what comes as it manifests itself.

You are enough. You are fitted to your time, the product of all that came before and the creator of what will be. You are never going to feel like a success every day, but when the pieces come together you can show yourself an exceptional master of your time and place. How can you make it through the doldrums to the swift winds and fair seas? How to avoid the disheartening of the bad days, how keep the dark moods from dragging you down?

Remember. Remember what you've seen— hold onto the triumphs and mountain peaks, the days of mastery and moments of clarity. When disappointments come, resist the urge to latch onto the feeling of despair as if it will last forever. You've seen your friends in direst straits and their inevitable rebound—allow yourself the logic of at least as much a chance of redemption as they receive. Take the longer view.

You are neither the sharpest tool in the drawer, nor the dullest hatchet in the shed. You are at the top of your game as often as the next fellow and you NEED to give yourself the acknowledgement you deserve. If you are ever kind to others when they are at their lowest, then it shouldn't be so terribly difficult to be as just to yourself. You've heard it said,

"Tough times don't last, tough people do." Well I've got a better one for you "Everyone goes through tough times, but only those who retain their dignity and common sense come out of the rough spots no worse for the wear."

You are enough. You are smart enough, kind enough, strong enough, resilient enough, resourceful enough, talented enough, educated enough, prepared enough, positive enough, humble enough, careful enough, hardworking enough, pretty enough, young enough, mature enough, realistic enough, and worthy of success.

Enough. Embrace it. You are enough.

I GRADUATE IN 1985. *I have no memory of what political sentiments where swirling when I walked across that stage to accept my high school diploma, but I'm relatively sure emotions were not running at the fever pitch they are right now. When graduation day 2017 rolled around, I thought about the students who were walking out into this wild world of contradictions and falsehoods, and I needed to put down a few thoughts about the importance of the day and how it could be placed in a context—regardless of the political atmosphere in which it existed.*

TRANSITIONS

The key events in your life— those pivotal moments against which you will measure your existence for all time to come— happen swiftly and are gone before you know it. Your marriage, graduation, birth of a child, death of a parent, major career change— these and more represent portals through which we are transported and transformed. It will always be "Before I graduated. . . After we got married. . . During the transition to my new job." You may not be meaningfully changed, but you have a new ruler by which to measure time.

Every time I witness another graduation, I am struck by the hope and joy that most young graduates feel. It is written on their faces. They can feel the world change around them, and themselves change with it. I am no longer a "music student," I now and a "Music graduate." I am no longer a young striver, I now have achieved that thing for which I strove. I am emboldened, emblazoned with a new set of letters after my name, burnished by the stress of the trials through which I've come, rough edges sanded down, and a fresh shine on my surface gleaming.

Perhaps the hardest part of taking these abrupt turns on our path is making sure that we have truly learned the lessons. You have the knowledge, but have you truly assessed and accepted its significance? What does graduation signify?

I am just a guilty as the next person of having made the cynical statement "all that X degree really shows is that you can endure torture and jump through flaming hoops to reach a goal." While there is a grain of truth to this jaded nugget, it ignores the central truth of every academic accomplishment— each degree or milestone on the way to the perfection of who you are is UNIQUE to the person making the journey. Only you really know what truths you've learned, what old thoughts you've relinquished, what demons or deficiencies you've conquered—and it is a totally novel experience from any before it.

Only in graduate school entrance exams did I finally realize what knowledge I had made a permanent part of my psyche. Only in my first college teaching experiences was I able to truly discover what parts of my craft I was sincerely an exemplary practitioner of. Only after trying to improve a degree program I supervise did I become aware of the merits and shortcomings of the programs through which I had passed. Each experience enriches and assesses those preceding it, leading us higher, broadening our field of vision, sharpening our abilities to ascertain truth.

Graduates, you will only feel and confirm your "changedness" as life proceeds forward. Sometimes you will catch the realization in time to appreciate it, other times it will be long gone before you are able to grasp its significance. Take the time to feel. Take the time to reflect. Use the time you are given to soak in the goodness of what you've been given and what you have given yourself. Be grateful — to God, to yourself, your parents, teachers, friends, the universe, and to time itself for allowing you to pass this way. This moment is gone in an instant and you will never pass this way again. You are changed, we are changed, eternity is changed. Congratulations.

"GATHER YE ROSEBUDS WHILE YE MAY, *olde time is still a flying. And that young flow'r which smiles to day, tomorrow will be dying."* Herricks's poem is as true today as in the 16th century when it was new. I'm still thinking about the students graduating during the "winter of our discontent" and I wanted to say one more thing before it left me.

DO IT NOW

I spent years paying off bills from adventures I experienced— some were necessary for my career (degrees, training), others were my choice at the time (travel, books, REAL adventures), and regret NOTHING! While I was advised to "take some time off from school and make some money," "you can go to graduate school later if you need it," and "skip those trips to Europe, you can't afford it right now," and "you should be focused on saving for retirement," I ignored them all and did what I believed would yield the best end result. That end result being an educated, experienced, informed, and curious mind. I still have student loans— and they are just fine.

Some say there has to be a happy medium between "doing it now" and "saving for later" but friends, we have no guarantees of a later, we cannot see the future, TOMORROW IS NOT PROMISED.

I backpacked across Europe—14 countries—in 1990. Other times, I traveled to Italy, Austria, England, Spain, France, Belgium, Netherlands, Germany, Slovakia, Czech Republic, Croatia, Slovenia, Portugal, Denmark, Lichtenstein, Poland, Estonia, Latvia, and more! Some places twice or three times—because the opportunity arose and I could not tell my present self "No, you'll have to do this later!" If I waited until I could have afforded to do these things, I would never have gone—even now, with tiny amounts of money in my possession, my body would be unable to make some of those trips. My dear friend who traveled abroad with me in 1996 is now deceased—he would have missed it! My friends who traveled with me in 1997 are no longer physically able to go—they would have missed out! It had to be done THEN!

I bought my first house at 21 and renovated it—never been so scared or broke in my life! But I did it, and it was the right thing to do! In the end, I came out financially better off— but if it had bankrupted me, it was still necessary AT THE TIME.

If I had died before getting to travel, if I had allowed time to rob me of my stamina to build and improve or to walk long distances— that, my friends would have yielded a life poorly lived. People do not regret the things they did, they regret the things they DIDNT DO! "Be responsible," you say. "Think long term," some will offer." Avoid debt," is the admonition. Not me, not ever.

Seize NOW. Go NOW! Do NOW! Be NOW! Live NOW! As the old spiritual opines I "Wouldn't take nothing for my journey now!" In the end, the days spent, sights seen, people met, food tasted, wine savored, evenings spent, skies admired, memories made, adventures dared ALL MEAN MORE than your bank account or your residual inheritance left for people who should have earned it themselves.

Gonna go. Gonna live. Gonna smile. Gonna be and share — I can economize when I return, when the day has past, when my friends are gone, when nothing tastes good anymore anyway. Do not throw away your present! Live it! Whatever it is, go for it and wave to the naysayers as they fade into the distance behind you.

Thus endeth the rant! For now . . .

FALSE BRAVADO. *"I have the best words." "I will be the best jobs president." "I have all the best people." We are drawn to confidence—real or fake, it draws us in. Is it because we have accepted the lie that showing weakness is wrong, that vulnerability only leaves you open to being taken advantage of, that you should never admit mistakes? The lie of the 'self-made man" was probably illustrated best by President Barack Obama when he made the much-maligned but true statement "You didn't build that company alone! You didn't build the roads that carried your product, or the internet that sold it, or the infrastructure that supported your factory. Taxes from everyone in this country helped you build your business!" When we take that to heart and relieve the 'self-made' men of their luster, we can allow ourselves to be less-than-perfect and accept help now and then. This will also allow us to retain our esteem for those who reach out to us for help. They are also allowed to need assistance, because we have allowed ourselves.*

STRENGTH IN WEAKNESS

I am not good at being vulnerable, I never was. I am always ready and willing to help others but unwilling to ask for help myself. Completely comfortable with going it alone, I frequently attempt tasks all by myself that are better done with help—never expecting anything but success. Usually, these exercises in extreme self-reliance result in great triumphs that I can use to bolster my confidence for future ill-advised shows of independence. But now and again, the experience results in an injury or defeat that makes me question my ground rules. There is great fortune in these misfortunes. Without the small failures, I would doubtless be propelled into a truly historic mess in the future due to my fatal flaw. I'm glad to have failed and I'm trying to learn.

We learn most when we traverse territory we never planned to enter. The fresh perspective is invaluable and infuses us with new ideas and great, unexpected energy. I never take sick days, I'm almost never truly sick— but artificially enforcing this God-given advantage upon myself has made me careless and caused me to be unwell. The self-fulfilling prophecy ultimately ceases to come true.

When I inevitably do contract an illness, it takes everything in me to admit it and stay home— and often, I put it off until I am far sicker than would have been necessary if I'd been less obstinate and just given in at the first sign of weakness. The thing is, when I finally do the right thing and admit to needing rest and help from friends, they always step right up and make me see the folly of my hesitancy to admit my need for others.

Thank you, friends, for being there for me, and thank you, life, for teaching me about the strength of weakness.

IT IS NOT ENOUGH. *It is simply not enough to enumerate Trump's MANY faults. We have to recognize and enumerate our own. Why? Because recognizing faults in others is dismissively easy, in yourself, not so much. If we really believe in doing the right thing, and not just in running down those we disagree with, we have to point out our own flaws and endeavor to correct them—just as much as identifying the MULTITUDINOUS shortcomings of Big Orange. After all, the whole world can see those.*

PATIENCE

I struggle. I struggle every day, with being patient. I know my struggle has been good for me, I can see the effects. People say to me frequently "You are SO patient!" But they can't see my insides, they can't hear me mentally screaming "For the love of God, could you please hurry up?!" Or "Sweet baby Jesus, I've explained this fifty times—were you even listening!?" Yep, the only real accomplishment I've gained with my struggle is masking my internal IMpatience— but you know what? That has been more than half the battle.

Other struggles are:

- What to do with myself over breaks (Christmas, Summer, etc.) I'm fine as long as I can have a building or writing project— but if I don't, LOOK OUT!

- Cooking a reasonable amount of food —there are just two of us after all and we are NOT good with leftovers. Luckily I have at least one old friend who loves good leftovers and never tires of my offerings.

- Buying things for the right reason. I will hold out like a miser on something I sincerely need, but then break the bank on some frivolous trinket when I am weak (or bored). Retail therapy is NOT the answer. (Unless how to go bankrupt is the question)

- Knowing how much to call on friends. Since I am a notorious introvert, I seriously respect people's privacy and I always feel like I'm intruding when I call —and I never, NEVER just drop in. Now, mind you, I am not offended when anyone calls me, or simply drops by, but I carry the distinct feeling that my own call or visit is somehow "disturbing" people.

- Understanding that there is enough. Money, particularly. When I was a twenty-something, I could not have cared less about money "O well, I'll go out and make some more tomorrow!" I would always say. Now, like some old Scrooge, I worry and fret anytime the amount of money in the bank drops below my imaginary minimum—and I can tell you the exact moment that every payday for the next year occurs. We are not broke—we are not even remotely poor, but to hear the voices in my head you would think we live in a railroad car and forage for berries in the woods each night for dinner.

- Going to the doctor when I need to—it's like admitting I've been bad or something, I have to be MISERABLE to be convinced to go. I really can't tell you why.

Now, don't you feel better about your hang-ups and shortcomings? We all have them, and I'm just not going to hide mine anymore. Maybe, if we all know about them, it'll be easier to find a solution to them.

TRUMP HAS NO REAL FRIENDS. *It is the ultimate irony that his minions are chosen because they agree with him (and are therefore experts in whatever phantom field he sets them over), and they then become seen as his "friends." But one slight deviation from the Trumpian script and "friendship" goes right out the window! Rex Tillerson was this towering genius who was going to "save" (read dismantle) the State Department. THEN, someone suggested that Tillerson was smarter than Trump and the claws came OUT. Trump would challenge him to an IQ test "anytime." Sheesh . . . so much for friends. Omorosa was this miracle goddess who showed that black Americans really were Trump supporters after all (barf), and then, when she had outlived her usefulness, OUT she goes (with concomitant Security escort). Friends are important, but only if they are real.*

FRIENDS

Who are your real friends? Do you have any? How many do you need? How would you know if they weren't?

There are people who think that every person they meet is a friend. Some people think anyone who is nice to them is a friend. Others feel like their only friends are those who've known them since birth. We are taught, in this culture, that the person with the most friends wins life—look at social media—how many "friends," how many followers?

The truth is, very few people are really your friends. I'm not even using the term "true friends," just the basic term. We have manufactured a society where beauty, popularity, wealth, trinkets, fame, food, novelty, sensuality, obliviousness, and any fleeting pleasant feeling is set on a pedestal and pursued as though it were a true virtue.

Friends share values, they share histories. Friends share tragedies, triumphs, accomplishments, failures, other friends. Friends support friends and shelter them from others and from themselves. Friends want the best for us— they forego pleasures, honors, and benefits for themselves in order to support, comfort, and promote their friends.

Can you identify one true friend? One? If so, you are luckier than nearly everyone you know—why? Because the world is made up of the people I described up front. People whose friends "make them laugh," gossip with them, drink with them, do drugs with them, complain about their problems together, commit crimes together— or a million other circumstances creating the illusion of friendship. But real friends have given you something meaningful—or given up something meaningful for your sake. They've seen you at your worst—and stayed. They've been abused—and stayed. Real friends have made mistakes and made up for it.

S. TIMOTHY GLASSCOCK

Friends have been given every reason to leave your worthless, flawed, ungrateful, cruel, thoughtless, selfish, unkind, paranoid, depressed, dysfunctional, and self-centered carcass behind. But they stayed.

Got one of those? Fall to your knees and thank the Lord— and don't ever mistake one of those other cheap imitations for the treasure that is a real friend.

TRUMP SUPPOSEDLY VALUES LOYALTY. *Above all else. It's really one of the most specious claims they could make. Loved Bill and Hillary Clinton—LOVED them—said innumerable documented positive things about what great people they were, until he needed to run on a Republican platform. He even called Bill Clinton to ask if he should run! Then, THEN it all went south. Donated money to Hillary's senate campaign, then, "Crooked Hillary!" His support for and later denigration of a litany of politicians is staggering: Mitt Romney, John McCain, Lindsey Graham (against, and then for), Mitch McConnell, Paul Ryan—the list is interminable, I shan't go on. But loyalty is supposedly his pinnacle. Loyalty to Trump is the real goal, and anything that smacks of correcting him can land you in the wilderness of his disdain.*

ON LOYALTY

"What's wrong with the world today?" Can you think of 50 answers to that? I can cover them all in one word. Loyalty.

S. TIMOTHY GLASSCOCK

The great Molly Ivins used to say the number one rule in politics (in Texas anyway) was "You got to dance with them what brung ya." My grandmother would have said "Remember which side your bread is buttered one." Well, just like the most recent gospel readings in the lectionary have been leading with "You have heard it said. . . But I say unto you . . .," I am going to modify both of these venerable adages.

Loyalty is remembering those who have helped you but is also remembering those who have no one to help them. You were helped, now you must help. MUST. When you witness wealthy people, who care nothing for the poor, you are witnessing the ultimate act of disloyalty.

Loyalty is indeed knowing who is likely to do things advantageous to your interests, but more importantly knowing who is likely to do things advantageous to the poor and helpless. Given intelligence, given education, given a good upbringing, given proper nutrition, given civil rights, given proper health care, given human dignity, given the right of self-determination, how can you deny any of these things to others?

Loyalty is never selfish, never cruel, never thinks the worst of strangers. Loyalty is true to friends, true to country, but true to all people of good will. How can you want the best for people known to you and not realize that others deserve the same goodwill—after all, they are known to, and loved by someone—and if not, then they deserve it all the more.

A TRUMP DIARY

Be loyal. Practice loyalty. Dance with them what 'brung' you, remember the butter on your bread, and remember that you can bring others to the dance and add butter to the bread of those who would otherwise go without.

We have enough, we are saved— we need no more, we need no further saving. It's time to pass it on. It's time to show our loyalty.

JOBS, JOBS, JOBS. *This presidency is about jobs! Of course, the recession was fixed by the last president and unemployment is basically the same as President Barack Obama left it, but anyways . . . Maybe the reason we can't get "full employment" (whatever that means) is because we haven't given employers everything they could wish for—like the rescinding of all labor laws, or destruction of unions, or doing away with the minimum wage, or making it easier to send jobs to Mexico and China, or? Well, all that is in the works, so just hang tight. It'll get done, if the president can stay out of prison. In the meantime, I had a few words for young (and not-so-young) people about finding a job. It sounds a little preachy now, but I'm not changing it. It was inspired by listening to some of the most clueless young laggards I've ever known kvetch about their jobs (or lack thereof).*

GETTING A JOB

Two students asked me today—not 15 minutes apart—how they could get a job when they graduate. This is not the only answer, but it's mine. And I'm sticking to it!

A TRUMP DIARY

<u>The young (or clueless) person's guide to getting a job:</u>

'DO's

- Show up to wherever they will let you—part time job, volunteer agency, wherever — & DO THE WORK OF A FULL-TIMER.

- Be nice to people—NOT just the boss

- Be informed, know the ins and outs of the organization. No one anywhere wants to clean up after your messes and half-done work. They don't want to hear "I didn't know, I'm just a part-timer." The answer to that one is "That's right, and that's ALL you are ever GOING to be."

- Do all the work you can and ask for more. Find jobs to do that they didn't even know NEEDED to be done.

- Do the work better than anyone has ever done it and act like it was nothing. NOTHING. If people notice you, say "thanks" and move on to the next awesomely over-perfected and unexpected masterpiece of labor you can accomplish.

- Make yourself INDISPENSABLE. Make sure they wouldn't know WHAT to do without you. This is the linchpin of your success.

- Make sure everyone KNOWS how much you LOVE your work at this agency and that it is the single greatest place on the EARTH.

'DO NOT's

- Complain. There are plenty people doing that job. . .

- Treat your part-time job as if it is secondary in importance to everything else in your life. The dumbest, least competent, and most pedestrian individuals on earth are doing this—and everyone is SICK of it.

- Be a pain, constantly asking for exceptions to rules. This is the best way to make sure everyone NOTICES that you don't deserve a real job

- Take a sick day every time you feel the least bit tired or draggy. This is scrub mentality and it signals that you want to be in a subservient position until you retire or die—people who love their job NEVER miss, they show when they are *dying*, and colleagues have to tell them "GO HOME!"

- Allow yourself to be caught bad-mouthing your part-time job. Tell everyone, "Yeah, I'm just hanging out there 'til something better comes along—it's a real shit hole!"

- Antagonize people who are already full-time there. Be sure and let them know that you think you are better than they are, they love that, and it endears you to them. The boss will soon notice that everyone gags when they see you. No one adds an employee like that.

- Be fake. Older people can spot a fake from SPACE. Be real, be honest, and don't blow smoke up the boss's ass. (ask someone what that means)

- Be unreliable. It's the first line on a termination form.

- Ask to be paid every time you do so much as a minute's work. If you are not willing to do a few things for free, you will never get paid to do anything.

Hope this helps someone. It comes from nearly 40 years of experience. I know it works—I've used it OVER and OVER, and I've been very happy with the results. You're welcome.

"LOOK AT THAT FACE!" *No one can accuse me of being a fan of Carly Fiorino. I thought she was about the nastiest lady politician I had witnessed—and I don't feel necessarily good about acknowledging that fact—but to go after her for her looks was more than a bit shocking to me. This was one of the first inklings we had that Trump was indeed as crass as he appeared. We shouldn't be surprised that Trump felt it was ok to run down someone for their appearance since he has done it before, but we also shouldn't be surprised due to the fact that our whole culture has embraced the mindless acquisition of money as a virtue, and the ridiculous practice of equating looks with personality as two natural facets of the growth of class elitism. Our society allows people to be portrayed as virtuous because of success, and successful because of beauty. Both these tendencies are loathsome and are poisoning public discourse on a daily basis. Beauty pageants, a practice that should have rightfully been banned before the advent of the 21ˢᵗ century, and the continual fat-shaming of anyone and everyone in the public eye—both should let us know that our sickness is real. You can be too rich, and you can be too thin. When will be accept people as they are? When we accept ourselves as we are.*

EMBRACING ENOUGH

Enough! Enough, already! I have enough. You have enough—though others have more, you are gifted with sufficient abundance for your life, if you accept it.

Why must we compare ourselves with people whose backgrounds and talents bear no resemblance to our own? Why do we devalue the blessings we've been afforded because they are different from someone else's? There are people with MUCH more money than I have, but I have come through tremendous trials to achieve what I have and should recognize the grand feat that is my success.

I am not as thin as some people, I have some health challenges. But for where I have been and the troubles I've survived, I'm doing great! My health is good enough to cause me to be grateful and give me reason to accept it as enough.

There are people with a higher profile in my field than me. But the place I hold is rewarding to me and gives me satisfaction in my work. I am happy to do what I do and to be recognized for it in the ways and proportion that I find myself receiving. It is enough. Other people get more public notice than I do, but perhaps they NEED that recognition more than I do— I don't crave it. If they need it, I am happy that they receive it. What I am getting is enough.

There are multiple sophisticated studies that show how achieving great wealth makes people more callous to the needs of their fellow man, greedier, more impatient, less caring, more self-centered and self-serving. If achieving large sums of money causes that phenomenon, could it also be true with other types of abundance? Would getting greater recognition, or friends, or professional success also lead to a lessening of empathy for my fellow man?

I know that the pursuit of fame, the pursuit of recognition, the pursuit of professional prominence causes people to ignore the importance of bestowing these graces on others—the obsession with "me, me, and ME" tends to blind a person to the shallowness of their interactions with others. And while the obsessed person won't notice their changed behavior, those around them most assuredly notice it—and can be brutal in their ridicule of the needy individual. It's hard not to notice a self-obsessed person, and it is often fairly comical. That is not something I desire—do you? I think I'll try harder to accept my "enough."

I was caught once griping about some nit-picky, silly little slight I felt I had received at work. A very wise person listened to me, and after enough time to commiserate with me so as not to seem unsympathetic, told me something I now consider a golden quote. She said, "Go to work, do your job, and then GO HOME!"

I have meditated on this wisdom and concluded that its simplicity is prodding me to accept "Enough." Doing my job, receiving what I receive, and retreating to my happy place— it truly IS ENOUGH.

I am trying. It is enough. Yours is enough too. Examine it closely, you'll see.

ACCEPTANCE IS NECESSARY. *This is where we are. This is the way things are going to be for a while—how long we don't know, but a while. Once we accept that, we can start to change the situation. But acceptance is necessary. Here we are, and all we have is what we make of it. We have to go on from here.*

WHAT WE HAVE

The world is not perfect, but it is what we have. We spend untold amounts of energy lamenting the bad in the world but take for granted all the good. Is it possible that we find bad because that's what we are seeking?

When you look at what others have and compare it to what is yours, are you looking for evidence of bounty in your life, or are you looking for something to complain about? It seems we compare ourselves to others for two reasons: to indict THEM for not being as (X) as we are, or to indict OURSELVES for not being as (X) as THEY. Neither of these is constructive. The only acceptable comparison of persons is that which you use to encourage gratitude in yourself or others. "Your life is not so bad! Look at the people who have to (X) to get by—you're certainly doing better than they are! Be thankful you have (X)!"

People are not perfect, but they are what we have. Your friends may not be utterly gracious at all times, but sometimes they get it right. Your family may not live in perfect *sympatico*, but when they get along, it is a great joy to everyone. Your co-workers may not be the most conscientious, the most energetic, the most innovative, the most gracious, but they can often surprise you with any of these things! People minus their demons and shortcomings would be pleasant, but they would also lack the depth of character and ability to forgive YOUR failings that our real flesh-and-blood co-inhabitants of this earth possess. Do they often fail to utilize their empathy? Yes. Do you?

Your job, your talents, your wealth—they may not be what you wish they were, but they are what you have. Could you have more money? Could you be recognized more widely? Could you have a better job? Yes. Is it worth sacrificing your peace when it may never happen? No.

I was once chasing "prominence," "recognition," "renown," and it seemed the most important thing in the world to me. One day, I suddenly saw through the clouds. The veil was lifted, and I could see that I was chasing someone else's life, someone else's fame or success. It wasn't what I needed to be happy, it was what I saw others enjoying and thought it would make me happy too. There is, firstly, no guarantee that anyone you see appearing contented is actually as they seem—and, secondly, absolutely no guarantee that what they have would create one iota of happiness within your heart. So why would you convince yourself to seek it? The first step is saving yourself from this faulty quest. The second? NOT trying to save anyone else. It cannot be done. Everyone arrives at readiness at their own pace and nothing you can offer (unsolicited) will hasten their enlightenment. "When the student is ready, the teacher will appear."

I see friends striving mightily for goals that I do not understand—goals I think are wrong for them and they will either never achieve or will achieve and be sadly disappointed in their ability to satisfy. But THAT, that striving after mammon, that fruitless longing, that fool's errand that robs you of peace IS THE STORY OF HUMANITY. You cannot explain it so that people will stop chasing it and improve their lives—learning this lesson IS LIFE. IS. LIFE. They can only do it themselves. What if it takes them until the very end? Then it does, it just does. There is no other way to learn it, and the lesson is important enough that, whether learned as a young person and given a rich long life to savor it in, or learned as a dying person and realized on your death bed, it is enough.

Do the best you can with what you have, because what you have is ALL you have. There may well be no more. Tomorrow is promised no one, and how senseless to spend your last days longing for that which never was, is not now, and never will be?

What is life? Not perfect. Not ideal. Not convenient. Not wholly satisfying. Not bliss. Not capable of being transformed into any of these. Bloom where you are planted—that is triumph! Taking what you were given, with all its advantages and disadvantages, and somehow making it work. Making it with what you have.

What is life? It is what we have.

SELFISHNESS IS IN STYLE. *Trump supporters, who cling to a dubious notion that they are somehow representative of Christianity, are notoriously selfish! The government is taking their money, never mind generations of Americans have paid their taxes completely willingly, knowing that streets, sewers, airports, railroad lines, telegraph and telephone infrastructure, social safety net programs for the poor and elderly—all of these legitimate functions of any government—are reliant on taxes. They, however, resent every penny. Trump himself claims huge largess—claims to give "millions" to charity each year. No one can quite find any evidence of this charitable activity but take his word for it (you have no other choice since his tax returns are more private than any modern president). We shouldn't be using American assets to help refugees or immigrants (legal or otherwise) because we have poor people here who should come first. THEN, you try to get them to agree to any program that helps our resident poor . . . good luck with that. We love our veterans! Boy do we love them! We aren't really happy about spending any money on them, but we love them. More money for arms, more money for military readiness—but for the VA? For homeless vets? There just, "isn't enough money". The republican congress wrote a tax bill that slashed MILLIONS*

from the budget to give ultra-wealthy folks and corporations a tax break but left the Children's Health Insurance Program (CHIP) unfunded. Orrin Hatch said, "There's just not enough money!" Really? I wonder WHY?!

GIVING JOYFULLY

I do not celebrate the cult of stardom. I do not use the word "!amazing!" (It must have the two exclamation points, it's too exuberant for just one!) I don't do heroes or idols, they are just so boring. I shy from hyperbole (except for comedic effect). Why? Because I believe some of the greatest things I've ever seen have been done by ordinary people—people who may never be called "the greatest X" or "one of America's finest X."

Let me explain. Humans blow things out of proportion and then they run with the metaphor. "I saw so-and-so do such-and-such and she WAS AMAZING!" Now person two rushes out and must see it also and agrees—and the trend snowballs. This sells a lot of tickets or records or purses or seminars or memberships. BUT. Truly inspiring things happen every day—all around us! And these things are barely acknowledged.

One of my former students rescues abused animals and cares for strays, full time! One of my former students works with abused, neglected, or homeless youth. A friend of mine for many years now has helped found a church that is 100% affirming of LGBTQ people and welcomes in those cast aside by mainstream religion. Another, volunteers for "meals on wheels" full time in his retirement. Retired folks I know spend several days each week working at the Franciscan Shelter, feeding the homeless. A dear friend in her 90s still volunteers locally teaching English to Hispanic children and adults. An old friend goes daily to local libraries and reads to toddlers and grade-schoolers. These are my heroes. These are my idols. This is where I lavishly spend my superlatives—real people, doing not superhuman feats or artistic juggernauts, but simple everyday kindnesses that no one else wanted to do.

Now these are not the only people who restore my faith in goodness, who bring out my pride in humanity—there are others who do smaller things, but who are, nonetheless, heroes to me. . .

One of my students greets me with the most exuberant hello each day—and I don't know how I've gotten along without it until she arrived. One of my colleagues asks me if I'd like coffee EVERY TIME she makes it or goes to get some. A colleague and friend has adopted little tasks I used to do by myself and now handles them himself so that I can attend to other duties—without being requested to do so. One of my students assists me with communication to the other singers—of his own accord. A work-study student on our staff watches to see if any important task has been missed or neglected by her peers and then fixes it—on, or off the clock—no matter. I could go on for days!

All of these little contributions—just to MY life—not to mentioned what the same individuals are likely doing for countless others I do not witness are miracles to me because they are a witness to Giving Joyfully. Not out of guilt, not out of a sense of duty, not out of a desire for praise or notoriety, but just contributing in a material way out of sheer goodness and joy.

This habit is my personal goal. Could it be yours? Celebrate Giving Joyfully!

THE GOVERNMENT IS TOO BIG. Really?! You can look at the state of our environment, the number of homeless people on the streets, the levels of drug addiction, the amount of misunderstandings between people, the inequality between people of different "races", the disparity of compensation between men and women, the infant mortality rate, the incarceration rate, the country's dependence on foreign oil, the state of diplomacy throughout the world, etc, etc, etc, and conclude that we need government to do LESS?!?

DOING NOTHING

I find it so hard to do nothing. Boys and girls, the puritan work ethic put a real hurt on me— I'm an addict, to activity. And we all need to find it in ourselves to allow the mind and body time to just "be." However, while time off from "busyness" is not only acceptable but necessary, there are situations where doing nothing is morally reprehensible. Here are a few:

Social injustice, bigotry, publicly aired hatred. This type of occasion does not offer anyone a free pass— you're against it, or you're a part of it. We all witnessed one of the lamest, most ill-advised, and most morally bankrupt reactions to this first instance from our erstwhile commander-in-chief immediately following the Charlottesville incident. No, Mr. Trump, "many sides" won't cut it. You're anti-Nazi, or you're a Nazi. End of story. In more recent statements, you've pretty much removed all doubt as to where you fall on that spectrum. Congratulations, or should I say "Sieg Heil"?

Human suffering. The Texas flooding brought on by Hurricane Harvey has shown us the worst kind of devastation that climate change can bring. These days, if you're a politician, it's more about what you appear to be doing than what you are actually accomplishing— and Mr. Trump made a ham-handed attempt at being presidential during this, which we cannot perhaps criticize, since he evidently just has hams for hands and can do nothing differently. The rest of us should donate, call legislators, and ride herd over this administration until they make good on their oh-so-readily offered promises.

The dismantling of our government. This administration has put more ne'er-do-wells in positions of power than Nero. If you were a crank who denied science, you now run whatever government science office you were working the hardest against. If you stood in the way of Justice, you're running an agency charged with upholding justice. If you spent years trying to outwit a particular government regulatory agency—you're likely running it. We can't stand by and watch this play out. Doing nothing is more unacceptable now than ever before. You don't have to be a rocket scientist to run a science agency (although other administrations have thought this was at least worth trying), but you must at least be actually committed to the best interests of science and not tearing down the progress we had until now. You don't have to be an Audubon, or a Roosevelt, or a Bernheim to manage public lands—but you do have to at least BELIEVE in public lands and be committed to their preservation. Robber barons need not apply!

It is the God-given duty of all true Americans to stand up at every opportunity and to defeat this administration before it destroys every bit of promise our country has left. Give them hell. And let the impeachments begin!

TWO WOLVES. *An old saying goes: "Inside each of us are two wolves, one that is good and kind, and one that is evil and hateful. How do we know which one will win? Easy! The one you feed." Now, the provenance of this story is in doubt—some say it is Native American, either Cherokee or Eskimo—other say that it is an extrapolation of an old Billy Graham sermon. But regardless of its origin, the basic truth is the same: the part of your nature you feed or encourage will be stronger and "win" the battle inside you. Trump feeds the bad wolf. Perhaps that's an understatement. Trump gorges the bad wolf and positively starves the good one. "Nasty Woman," "Little Marco," "Lyin' Ted," "Crooked Hillary," "Boring Jeb," "Mexican rapists and drug dealers," "shit-hole countries,"—all this and more show us the side of his dual nature (if the good wolf is even still with us) that Trump is feeding. Just like you don't have to actually smoke to receive the negative effects of cigarette carcinogens, second-hand negativity is also dangerous. Just as Villanova study found that negativity in the workplace stifles creativity, breaks down communication, gets in the way of teamwork, and pummels the life out of motivation, so also can negativity in your life—even just that which you watch on television—creep in and sour all the positives you enjoy. To counteract the effects of Trump's*

nastiness, I had to sometimes un-plug and step away to get back my bearings and re-align my positive self.

FEEDING THE SOUL

The daily grind is not the place where we find our inspiration. The world comes at us 90 miles per hour and we find ourselves playing firefighter—rushing to address fires as they break out and having not a moment to truly reflect on what we have seen and done, or to consider whether it was the appropriate response or simply the only response available. This is not a choice—we really MUST react as life unfolds and, barring life-altering exigencies, those decisions must suffice on a daily basis.

This does not mean that we need never reflect, analyze, or evaluate—we must, but recognizing the pressures of everyday life, we should expect that time away from the usual is our only hope of an honest personal "inventory." This realization is important for several reasons: the obvious one described above, as well as some less obvious ones I want to examine.

Daily hand-to-hand existence does not feed the soul—as much as we talk the lingo about "my job is the perfect job," or "I love what I do," the truth is that no job, by itself, provides automatic personal nurture if we are really getting things done. Stress and frustration steps in and robs us of that joy. We feed our soul, not as a selfish endeavor, for in truth there are no selfish moves if we do as we are intended (to help others), but as intended good for the universe. Only a fully nourished, mentally rested, and consciously alert soul can maneuver the path of the greatest good. The starving soul may clumsily help a few people as it gropes through its paces—it may even understand some of the good it does, but the depleted and distracted soul can never reach its full potential and cause the titanic waves of human benefit it was intended to create as a fully realized humanity. We therefore must achieve this state of spiritual readiness by stepping away and giving our minds and spirits what they need—rest, peace, comfort, joy, creature comforts to a certain extent. Then, THEN we can reach the heights we are expected to scale by the author of life.

Step away, turn off the phone, go incognito, be unreachable, rest, hug someone (or several someones) for extended periods. Renew, review, revise, reboot, retreat, and then RETURN.

THE CONSTANT NEGATIVITY IS DEAFENING.
*Not a day goes by that this president doesn't embarrass himself
and us all in some totally unbelievable way, giving way to
a feeling of hopelessness, to the sense that things will never
be "normal" again. But Trump is NOT America. Trump is
not a reflection of our country. He is a reflection of the lesser
angels of our nature, the dark side of democracy, the failures
of pluralism. Instead of the representing our highest ideals, the
triumph of our greatest aspiration, Trump represents the side of
our electorate we've been trying to forget—bigotry, xenophobia,
insular thinking, selfishness, greed, isolationism, the national
superiority complex as public policy. We have to remember that
a happier day will dawn. A day will return when the attitudes
and behaviors of Donald J. Trump will be relegated to the
dustbin of history and America resplendent can once again
emerge as a leader on the world stage and our true democratic
values will once again drive our policy. Will we ever be perfect?
Of course not, but we can certainly, once again, be better than
this!*

TOUCHING BASE

I am a nester. Wherever I go, I have a command center, a nest, a place that is uniquely mine where I retreat to and gain my strength before striking out and conquering. Like Superman's 'Fortress of Solitude,' I have to have a place to hide and regain my moorings. I have renovated numerous houses, built a cabin, customized my decks and sunrooms—all, it seems, to provide that special place of belonging.

But as much as my childhood clubhouses, and homes, and cabins are my touchstone and retreat, my original place of respite is the earth—that is dirt, the ground, *terra firma*. I was engaged in farming and gardening from my birth. My mother carried me through the fields when they were working in tobacco and let me play in the dirt when they were gardening. I am never quite so at home as when planting or harvesting some crop. I planted gardens, set tobacco, baled hay, mowed yards, picked peppers and beans and blackberries.

That connection to the earth is a comfort to me and a reminder of the essential place gardening and farming hold in human existence. We have nothing that the ground doesn't give us—our food, the animals we consume or live off (cows for milk and chickens for eggs), the minerals and metals with which we build, the trees that give us wood, the oil and gas we exploit for industry and travel. This is all, our life, the gift of the earth.

I always knew I was happier when I had contact with growing things, with humus (not hummus), and though I could not place why, it was palpable and absolutely real. Now we know that there are actually chemical and hormonal attributes to the soil that elevate our mood (we always knew that poor dirt farmers had to have more than their paltry earnings to make them smile). So, this fact confirms and justifies my lifelong yearning for soil and cultivation—makes my emotional need into a logical desire.

Return! Return is the most prevalent theme in literature, music, dance, everything. Things and people go away—and they return. The sun, the seasons, the rains, the birds, the storms, the flowers, the snows, our friends, relatives, our sanity, our happiness, our loves, our fortunes, our children—all go away, and hopefully, RETURN.

Come back to your senses, come back to God, come back home, lover come back, get back to basics, get down to ground level, retrieve your values, revisit your childhood, get back to where you once belonged! We love to travel, to leave, to explore—but OH, how we love to return! We are always returning. I am returning: to my roots, to my kin, to my senses, to my values, to my center, to the beginning, to the start, to my essence, to the earth. And our constant activity of leaving and the release of returning is a foretaste of that inevitable day when we shall make our final return to the ground from whence we came.

Genesis 3:19 "In the sweat of thy face shalt thou eat bread, till thou return unto the ground; for out of it wast thou taken: for dust thou art, and unto dust shalt thou return."

And that return will be the true homecoming— shared by us all. In the meantime, I am planting a garden today.

WAS THAT A MISSTATEMENT? *I sat in rapt anticipation as the president's press secretary (number three in a year) was asked if, since she had basically completely refuted the statement of the president, was she actually correcting him, or did he accidentally misspeak, or? What? There was absolutely no revealing answer forthcoming. No admission that the present position was any deviation from the previous absolutely contradictory statement, no indication that either statement was more correct than the other, nothing. It was as though the simple acknowledgement that anything had changed would constitute an admission of failure. You would think that an administration that had been proven wrong SO many times would have gotten used to it by now.*

FACING OUR FAULTS

No one is perfect. We all have our faults, and the only honest way to deal with that fact is to admit what they are and, while we certainly wish to improve, admitting that some of them are just "part of us."

What one flaw, tick, or habit would you change if you could? Not just an innocent tendency, but a real character fault—come on, everyone has at least one. Here's mine: I can be led into negativity. Not serious, bitter, conniving negativity—just bitchy, petty, catty, snarky gossip. There, I've said it. Well, I won't let myself off the hook that easily, I'll get more specific. I, as a rule, do not begin with negativity—I do not burst into a room with "you'll never guess what I just saw!" but if someone else does, I. Am. There. I can be counted upon to "ooh" and "ah" over the juicy details and to add little juicy touches if I know them and to thoroughly ENJOY a short interlude of *Schadenfreude*.

Now, I do not share this as something I am proud of. I am, instead, appalled at my glaring shortcomings—and I intend to move toward ameliorating this part of my personality. What do I want? Simple. I want to be able to encounter that person spreading bad news or innuendo and, gently, and not as a preachy or chastising censor, turn that conversation in a better direction. I. Am. Going. To. Try.

If we aren't personally involved in our own improvement, there will be none. I hope you won't judge my flaw too harshly, but I promise, my behavior is going to improve. Will you make that pledge with me—not on my fault, but one of your own? Let's become better people together. Share your shortcomings. If not with me, with someone. Tell a relative, a best friend (unless they are the one who leads you down the primrose path), go to confession, start a journal if it's just too embarrassing to share. You can do this. WE can do this!

THE EARTH IS NOT OURS. *It does not belong to us. We belong to the earth. The treatment of the Standing Rock Native American protesters who opposed the Keystone XL pipeline, showed what the Trump administration thinks of a stewardship-based view of our environment. The trashing of the infrastructure of our public land custodians show what the Trump administration thinks of preservation of public resources. The list goes on. Trump and his ilk have no sense of needing to preserve anything for future generations. The only thing they value is the profit that can be gained in the here and now. Well we know that we will not be the last people on earth. We are aware that, barring some nuclear catastrophe that His Royal Tan-ness has yet to provoke, there will be generations to come after us and we have a responsibility to protect what we have and leave it—in as pristine condition as possible—for whoever is next. This philosophy is not only appropriate for conservation purposes, it also helps us to keep in perspective what our true place in history is, and to keep from taking ourselves so seriously.*

PASS IT ON

Why is it that some people can do their work, step back and say "Ok, enjoyed that," and move on, while others keep standing around waiting for their Oscar? Some folks take the experience for what is was, cherish what they can, and look to the future—others finish each happening as if it must be either the pinnacle of all experiences or someone must be blamed. (Mind you, this blame will rarely fall on THEM, but rest assured, it WILL fall on SOMEONE.)

I believe the difference is whether we recognize the nature of our part in the grand scheme. Now, I can hear you saying, "Does ANYONE really understand how we fit into the 'grand scheme'?" Well, yes! It's not a great secret I'm discussing here—it's merely a very important dichotomy, and forgive me, but I must turn to sports to explain: there are individual races, and there are relays. That's it. That's the secret. Life, approached in the healthiest manner possible is NOT an individual race, it is a relay.

In individual races—100 yd dash, sprint, etc.—the person who starts is the person who finishes. If you win, you get a medal. If you don't win, you get disappointment. So, you can view your activity here as a series of high stakes individual events— where you are a winner or a loser— or you can view it, ALL of it, as one great cosmic relay.

Let me explain. When I rehearse a choir and present a concert, first of all, how can anyone count an accomplishment like that as an INDIVIDUAL pursuit anyway? It is obviously a group endeavor. But EVERYTHING is a group endeavor.

Something President Obama said several years back that really resonated with me pertained to wealthy individuals paying taxes. He said, "You hear people saying 'Why should I pay taxes on this money? I built this company all by myself and I deserve the profits! But you DIDN'T build anything by yourself— you didn't build the roads that transport your product. You didn't create the internet where you marketed your goods. The utilities, water, electric, sanitation, necessary to support your factory and your distribution were all created by other people—and with taxes PAID FOR BY EVERYONE." Life is like that too.

The job where I function was here in some form before it was mine—even if it was new with my hiring, somebody facilitated that job creation and IT WAS NOT ME. I simply pick up where I am brought into this game and man my oar until it is no longer mine to row. And when I am done here, through retirement, migration to another post, or the ultimate moving on (dirt nap), SOMEONE ELSE will take up the reins, gather the torch from my hand, and continue. What a shame and a waste is my life if I fail to see the transient nature of my proprietorship of this thing called music making and think that the true ULTIMATE of all that is or will be is my latest accomplishment or failure! It is SO much BIGGER than that!

This race goes on, and on, and on! Through generation and eon, the March of humanity goes from artistic endeavor and from humanitarian triumph to innumerable new vistas we will never see! It is ours only to ride this pony until it is someone else's turn and, hopefully, hand off the reins a little better than we found them. The spirit of a relay also allows us to enjoy the fellowship of the whole human race in our attempts and to see the trajectory of greatness yet to come far beyond our ability to actually participate.

You can have your sprints, you can have your individual dash—I am MORE than satisfied with my small part in the unknowable middle of this huge cosmic relay! Good luck to us all!

THESE ARE DARK DAYS. *You cannot deny that each passing day seems a little less secure than the last one. Lies, damn lies, and false statistics—this president can use them like no other. But nobody gets away with it forever. I have great faith that justice will prevail, but OH how I wish it would hurry.*

ALWAYS DARKEST. . .

When? When is it always darkest? Before the dawn? Just before it goes completely black? Just when you think it can't get any worse? When things seem like they're mending, but then WHAM!?

A lot of us are reliving our memories of the 1970s when President Richard Nixon was being investigated from every angle and finally became so enraged and fearful that he fired Watergate Special Prosecutor Archibald Cox—and the nation, on both sides of the aisle, revolted. Regardless of your feelings about the 2016 election, you can't find anything positive to say about what's happening now. Republicans are split between old-line conservatives who are beginning to seriously question everything about this president, and neo-conservatives who keep thinking everything will be ok if we just sit tight and hang together. (Of course, you remember the old saw "Either we hang together, or we'll hang separately!"

Amid this whole turmoil and burgeoning crisis, we have to remember that the wheels of government move slowly and those of Justice even more so. Events of the last 24 hours won't reach their full-blown potential to reveal their importance for another day or so, and then we have to wait for reaction, and hopefully, resolution. Calmer heads will eventually prevail and, I believe, the majority of elected officials will recognize the need for a special prosecutor.

Aside: now, I'm no fan of this special prosecutor process. Nixon got one due to his own obfuscation and attempts at a cover up. Clinton got one because the GOP felt enough might be dredged up to swing the mid-terms. And there were definitely ugly parts to both of these. I cannot stand the sight of Kenneth Starr to this day— so I'm not rushing headlong into the arms of a special prosecutor—BUT— Mr. Trump and his compadres have neglected to learn the lessons of history. If you are guilty of something, you're going to be looked upon with much more mercy if you submit yourself to an investigation and then admit fault in any findings. If you LIE, if you DEFLECT, if you try to SABOTAGE, if you fling UNFOUNDED INVECTIVE, if you do attempt a COVER-UP. . . YOU. ARE. TOAST.

S. TIMOTHY GLASSCOCK

Let's go easy on the blaming of the unfortunate folks who hitched their hopes to Mr. Trump's wagon and keep the blame on the actual perpetrators in this poor, sad, inexperienced, unprepared, unvetted, unaware, and unlikely to survive administration. Today may very well be less the "end of the beginning." It's looking like the "Beginning of the end."

I'VE BEEN HARD ON TRUMP. *But every waking day makes me surer that it has been justified and that he will continue to prove my estimation of him correct. This is a dangerous man, and every day that he is any small part of our public discourse—let alone president—is a sad day. I don't see Donald J. Trump as an unredeemable figure—there is ALWAYS the possibility, however faint, that he will somehow see the error of his ways and try to change. But until that unlikely day, I will be here ranting to anyone who will listen that he must be stopped and that his devious alteration to our government must be eradicated as soon as humanly possible.*

THROUGH OLDER EYES

When young, we see the world as we hope it will be . . . Everything is just set in exactly the right place for our arrival and boy is this world going to take notice of us!

If we age, but do not mature, we see the world as we fear it might be. . . Disappointments cause us to begin looking over our shoulder muttering "what are they going to do to me today?!" In this circumstance, a person begins to see others as competitors, their opposing opinions as horribly misguided and probably formed with nefarious intent. The world becomes scary and we demonize anything that doesn't fall into our personal worldview as "what's wrong with the world."

But if we mature (those of us blessed with the years necessary to do so—a blessing to remember that not everyone gets), we begin to see the world as it really is. . . People are not simply good or bad but standing in a good or bad place for the moment. The world is neither waiting for us with a kind embrace nor hiding in ambush, instead it is here, doing what the world does, and circumstance, mated with our response to it, will decide what happens and where we go.

Attitude and effort. You've heard it many times—and it's a real truth. How we choose to see the world and what we're willing to do about it. You, dear friends and kind acquaintances, help me to see the world as a place of great possibility—a world where the confluence of goodwill and elbow grease can make a real difference. My goodwill is ever increasing. And while my capacity for elbow grease is, so far, undiminished, it is decidedly harder to motivate and lingers longer in the recovery room. So, I plan, as I age (god willing), to supplement my destined-to-wane capacity to work with a heftier shot of my ever-surging goodwill.

I'm hoping, like a youngster, that this will be enough. I'm accepting, like the ever-more-middle-aged soul I'm becoming, that, whatever the outcome, WE will make the best of it. And until that last shovel of earth is tossed on top of me, I will not stop trying to make a difference.

Printed in the United States
By Bookmasters